Larissa Behrendt is Professor of Indigenous Research and Director of Research at the Jumbunna Indigenous House of Learning at the University of Technology Sydney. She is a regular columnist for *The Guardian* and has published numerous textbooks on Indigenous legal issues. She is also the author of two novels: *Home*, which won the 2002 David Unaipon Award and the 2005 Commonwealth Writers' Prize for Best First Book (South-East Asia and South Pacific); and *Legacy*, which won the 2010 Victorian Premier's Literary Award for Indigenous Writing. She is the Ambassador of the Gawura Aboriginal Campus at St Andrew's Cathedral School in Sydney and a board member of the Sydney Story Factory, a literacy program in Redfern. She was awarded the 2009 NAIDOC Person of the Year and the 2011 NSW Australian of the Year.

Also by Larissa Behrendt

Fiction

Home

Legacy

Children's fiction

Crossroads

Non-fiction

Indigenous Legal Relations in Australia
    (with Chris Cunneen and Terri Libesman)

Indigenous Australia for Dummies

Australian Screen Classics: Rabbit-Proof Fence

*Achieving Social Justice: Indigenous Rights
    and Australia's Future*

Treaty
    (with Sean Brennan, Lisa Strelein and George Williams)

Discovering Indigenous Lands
    (with Tracey Lindberg, Robert J Miller and Jacinta Ruru)

FINDING ELIZA

*Power and
Colonial
Storytelling*

LARISSA
BEHRENDT

First published 2016 by University of Queensland Press
PO Box 6042, St Lucia, Queensland 4067 Australia

www.uqp.com.au
uqp@uqp.uq.edu.au

Cover and text design by Heather Menzies, Studio 31 Graphics, Inc.
Cover images: *Young Woman from Fraser Island, ca. 1899*, artist unknown,
John Oxley Library, State Library of Queensland Neg: 75998.
Portrait Sketch of Eliza Fraser, artist unknown, John Oxley Library,
State Library of Queensland Neg: 31364. Background image: DavidMSchrader/iStock.
Typeset in 11.5/15 pt Adobe Caslon Pro by Heather Menzies, Studio 31 Graphics, Inc.
Author photograph by Jonathan David Photography
Printed in Australia by McPherson's Printing Group

All attempts have been made to contact copyright licensees for permission
to reproduce material. If you believe material for which you hold rights is
reprinted here, please contact the publisher.

National Library of Australia
Cataloguing-in-Publication data is available at http://catalogue.nla.gov.au

ISBN
978 0 7022 5390 4 (pbk)
978 0 7022 5630 1 (ePDF)
978 0 7022 5631 8 (ePub)
978 0 7022 5632 5 (Kindle)

University of Queensland Press uses papers that are natural, renewable and recyclable products
made from wood grown in sustainable forests. The logging and manufacturing processes conform
to the environmental regulations of the country of origin.

for

Michael Lavarch

If not for other, there is no self.
If not for self, nothing is apprehended.

Chuang-tzu

CONTENTS

1

Once Upon a Time

SCHEHERAZADE'S WEDDING NIGHT was fraught with a particular peril. Convinced that women were unfaithful after a betrayal by his first wife, her new husband, King Shahryar of Persia, had ensured the fidelity of each subsequent bride by executing them the day after the wedding, thereby guaranteeing that they would not stray.

Scheherazade escaped this fate with a very powerful weapon: the art of storytelling. On her wedding night, she enthralled her husband with a story. But she did not conclude the tale. Instead, she left him dangling in suspense as dawn broke. He spared her life because of his deep curiosity about what happened next.

The following evening Scheherazade continued her story. She wove her tale throughout the night and, as the sun once again rose, left her husband craving to know more. She did the same the next night, and the next, and the next. If a story ended, she would begin a new one before the night was over, and the tales of *One Thousand and One Nights* are now testament to her time-honoured craft of storytelling.

At the end of those thousand and one nights, Shahryar had fallen in love with Scheherazade and she had borne him three sons. He had also grown wiser through the morals woven through her tales. Scheherazade's stories had not only saved her life but also made her husband a better man – and a better king. I like to think that she enjoyed life to a grand old age.

As a novelist, I am of course seduced by the idea that stories can be so powerful, can take such a hold over the listener and be transformative. But as an avid reader and as a regular visitor to the cinema and theatre, I know how true this is. Few pleasures in life feel more decadent than reading a book from cover to cover simply because you cannot put it down. Those books become like treasures – mine include *Blood* by Tony Birch, *Larry's Party* by Carol Shields, *The Guernsey Literary and Potato Peel Pie Society* by Mary Ann Shaffer and Annie Barrows, *True Pleasures: A Memoir of Women in Paris* by Lucinda Holdforth, and everything by Jane Austen, the Brontë sisters, Henry James and Charles Dickens. I can't imagine *not* having these books close by in my house; they feel like friends.

If further evidence is needed of the hold on our hearts that stories have, we might simply look at the way our favourite tales from childhood remain with us for the rest of our lives. I still have a copy of *Mog the Forgetful Cat*, as well as my copies of Enid Blyton's chronicles of the Famous Five and the Secret Seven. I didn't part with them when I grew up into the world of Nancy Drew and the Hardy Boys. And I still couldn't part with them when

I moved into the worlds of Mr Rochester, Mr Darcy and Colonel Brandon.

This book is inspired by one story that captured my imagination. It is the tale of Eliza Fraser, a white woman who was shipwrecked on an island off the east coast of Australia in 1836, and who spent a period of several weeks with the local Aboriginal people of that land. Like most stories that have a powerful impact, it is a simple one. A classic 'fish-out-of-water tale', as they might call it in the movie business.

I came across Eliza's story by a circuitous route. I had been aware of it in the vaguest of ways from sources I couldn't recall, but it came to mind when I was living in the prairies of Canada after finishing graduate school in the United States. In a little bookshop in Saskatoon I came across a copy of Sarah Carter's *Capturing Women: The Manipulation of Cultural Imagery in Canada's Prairie West*. Fresh from my doctoral studies in law, I usually dived into the Cultural Studies section at the bookshop to find something that would spark my interest but often left empty-handed.

But *Capturing Women* turned out to be a treasure trove. It included accounts of white women who had been living with the Métis in Canada of their own free will but who had found themselves described in newspaper reporting at the time as having been kidnapped. It had suited journalists and politicians to create an image of the Métis as savage and threatening. And getting the population excited and worried about the threat helped sell papers. (Not much has changed in the tactics of the newspaper world, it would seem.) But no amount of protestation from the women themselves altered the way that these stories were told in the popular press. Facts were troublesome when competing with a convenient and titillating fiction.

So I became curious to revisit the story of Eliza Fraser that I remembered as a comparable one of a white woman 'captured by cannibals'. I was interested to see whether Eliza's story fitted the model that Sarah Carter had identified. It turned out it didn't. The tale of Eliza Fraser was far more nuanced and fascinating. She became both a charismatic and an elusive figure. As I traced her through the books that had been written about her, I found her to be more and more intriguing with the discovery of each new layer and interpretation of what had happened to her.

Eventually it was not just Eliza's own story that would fascinate me. I became interested in the ways in which she had captured the imagination of so many others. She had been the subject of several fanciful accounts of her life and, in 1976, an even more fanciful film – *Eliza Fraser* was directed by Tim Burstall from a screenplay by David Williamson, and starred Susannah York as Eliza, Noel Ferrier as her husband and Australian icon Abigail as 'Buxom Girl'. These interpretations tended to highlight the drama of the white woman among savages, as well as the 'boys' own adventure' aspect of her rescue.

Eliza's story also inspired more thoughtful reflection, though no less romantic. Sidney Nolan had painted her – on all fours crawling through the sandy landscape – and he had managed to intrigue his then close friend Patrick White, who himself was inspired to write a novel, *A Fringe of Leaves*, based on Eliza's experiences. White, unsurprisingly, took a more complicated view of Eliza. He played with her background, making the character she inspired – Ellen – a woman who was elevated from the working classes through her marriage instead of someone who had always enjoyed middle-class privilege. Like Nolan, White saw the drama in the struggle Eliza would have had against nature and conceived this as a metaphor for our own internalised struggles. Although White appeared to have a sympathetic view of Aboriginal people, he did not create them as well-rounded characters. They were included as a canvas against which to explore Ellen's psychological journey.

And it was the role that Aboriginal people play in Eliza's story that quickly became of central interest to me. The Butchulla people are the traditional custodians and owners of K'gari (pronounced 'Gurri'), the place now known as Fraser Island. In the stories of Eliza's time with them, they are – especially the men – part of the danger she faces. They are nameless. They are stereotyped negatively. They are barbaric. And they have been constructed in this way to make the story more interesting. Otherwise, the plot isn't so gripping; the audience isn't captivated.

But more was at stake in these diverse accounts than just ensuring a ripping yarn. Eliza's story was put to use well beyond anything she would have imagined. And here is the resonance with Scheherazade and her storytelling. Scheherazade told captivating tales but she did not tell them just for the pure pleasure they gave. Her agenda was to keep her husband intrigued enough that her life would be spared. Along the way she also used the messages and morals implicit in her stories to educate her husband and to shape his values. She succeeded, reminding us that often there is a motivation – a politics – that accompanies the telling of any story.

> *... often there is a motivation*
> *– a politics – that accompanies*
> *the telling of any story.*

Eliza's story is rich with motives, most of them not intended by her but by others. In fact, so many people have used her story, appropriated it for their own purposes, that in the end it is hard to see who she really is. I have concluded over the years that we hardly know Eliza at all. She is often as elusive as the Butchulla are in the pages that recount her experiences.

This book begins with how Eliza's story was told, by whom and why. Excerpts from various accounts of her tale re-create the tones and styles of the time. I then explore the themes that give this tale its dramatic tension and look at the motivations behind some versions of her story.

From the colonists' perspective I turn to that of the Butchulla, bringing them out of the shadows. They have their own reflections about Eliza's time with them and the legacy she left, and the contrast in perspectives reveals a complex and intriguing example of cross-cultural conflict.

Two themes of this story hold a particular fascination for me. I am naturally interested in the way that the Butchulla women are portrayed. The Aboriginal men might be constructed as a danger but the women are also given the role of villains, being jealous of Eliza because she is white and therefore assumed to be more attractive. The Aboriginal women are stereotyped negatively – as promiscuous, as bad mothers, as vindictive.

Then there is the fear of cannibals. In Eliza's tale, and other captivity narratives from the United States, Canada and the Pacific, it is assumed that the indigenous people of each area are cannibals. It's part of their inherent danger. Yet there is little evidence of cannibalism in any of those places. The Butchulla certainly weren't into the business of eating each other, so why were they presumed to be? And why did Europeans imagine cannibals to be in every new place they went?

It is easy to look at Eliza's story today and see how these negative stereotypes of Aboriginal people are simplistic, racist and offensive. But a more stimulating and difficult question is raised by the use of positive stereotypes when representing Aboriginal people. If painting Aboriginal people as villains and their culture as barbaric is antiquated, isn't it the case that accounts of Aboriginal people in popular culture that employ positive stereotypes are automatically a good thing? Well, at the risk of sounding like I can never be happy – no, it's not. What harm, then, can be done by positive stereotypes?

Two instances in recent times provoke a response.

Elizabeth Durack was a well-established and respected artist in her own right when she invented the *nom de brush* of Eddie Burrup and attributed to him a new style of painting she developed. She invented not only the name but also a whole backstory of Eddie's life and worldview. Eddie was opposed to native title; he liked it better when the white people were in charge; he didn't trust half-castes. When Durack finally revealed that she was Eddie Burrup, she described the creation of this alter ego as an act of reconciliation and an essential part of her creative process. Looking at the choices she made about Eddie provides an interesting account of how a non-Aboriginal person sees an Aboriginal one.

Marlo Morgan spent thirty-one weeks on the United States bestseller list with her book *Mutant Message Down Under* after it was released by a commercial publisher in 1994. Morgan's account of her adventure in Australia, where she meets a lost tribe of Aboriginal people who give her a warning to take back to the rest of the world about the dangers posed to the environment, was a sensation not only with the New Age market but also with the wider reading public. Her Aboriginal tribe were quintessential noble savages, untouched by European culture; so in tune with nature were these people, they were telepathic. When the veracity of Morgan's book was questioned, she became defensive, stuck to her story and maintained that the Aboriginal people from Australia who questioned her didn't believe her because they were not real Aboriginal people.

These stories do not occur in a vacuum; they meander into our value systems and our institutions. Every time I explore the concepts in Eliza Fraser's story, I seem to find my way back to the legal implications that have flowed from the various accounts. As I am a lawyer by training, it is perhaps no surprise that I am interested in the way in which elements of each of these stories all seem to make some link with the legal system. Eliza's story was used to show that Aboriginal people were savage and in need of saving by missionaries, and because they were seen as not sophisticated enough to have property laws the same way the Europeans did, their land was there for the taking. The Butchulla link Eliza's time with them directly to their own dispossession.

Thinking about Eliza's story often makes me consider the way that my own profession uses storytelling, particularly in relation to Aboriginal people. On reflection, it is not surprising that I find links between storytelling and law. Law is another form of storytelling. It talks of precedent but it is also about competing narratives. Lawyers representing opposing sides in a case construct different stories of the facts to convince the judge or jury that their version is the correct one.

So this book is not just about Eliza's story; it is also about the other stories that I discovered and reconsidered in the wake of my fascination with her. Like all good stories, Eliza's shipwreck, her time with Aboriginal people and her eventual rescue raised more questions for me. Just like Shahryar waiting to hear Scheherazade's next twist, each time I think about one more permutation of the story, I want to know more.

2

The White Woman
Captured by Cannibals

THE WIND HOWLS on a dark night in newly charted waters. A ship is tossed around in a dangerous storm. As the waves pound, the rain lashes and the wind wails, a craggy reef tears at the ship's hull, pulling it apart. The rip is fatal; water cascades in and the hull fills quickly. The ship cannot be saved and the crew must abandon it.

It is 21 May and the year is 1836. The ship that has just become a victim of the Swain Reefs and been left to the sea is the *Stirling Castle*. By the time the storm subsides, the survivors are floating on the now-calm seas in two lifeboats, adrift off the coast of eastern Australia. Among them is Captain James Fraser, weak and ill, and his wife, Eliza.

The *Stirling Castle* left the bustling colonial port of Sydney only a week before the crew found themselves shipwrecked. They float in these waters for two months before setting foot on the world's largest sand island. This part of Australia will eventually become known as Fraser Island, named after the Captain of the doomed ship.

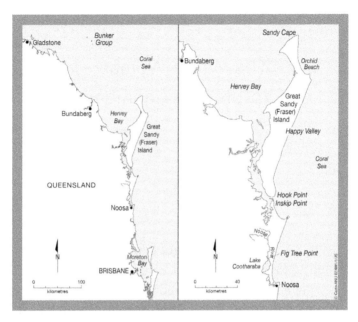

Fraser Island, the world's largest sand island, is located 15 km off the coast of Hervey Bay.
(Courtesy of the Australian National University, College of the Asia and the Pacific, CartoGIS)

Eliza has taken the first steps on her journey into Australian folklore. But her survival of the shipwreck is not the climax of this story; it is just the beginning. The heart of her story unfolds when she makes contact with the Aboriginal people who populate this land, and it is her alleged captivity by these 'brutal' and 'cannibalistic savages' and her eventual rescue that give her tale its compelling drama.

A sketch survives of Eliza Fraser. The drawing gives the impression of a petite, delicate woman. She has a strong, determined look, almost stern. She wears a bonnet and has a shawl wrapped demurely over her shoulders, depicting a certain middle-class purity and austerity, an embracing of the Victorian and Calvinist values that frowned upon excess. These were important values of the time and Eliza looks the embodiment of them. She is not a beauty, nor is she plain. She does not look warm or maternal, but neither does she look mean or unpleasant. She looks remarkably, well, unremarkable. She might not immediately strike you as someone who will be singled out in history or become an icon.

This portrait sketch is one of the few surviving images of Eliza Fraser. *(Artist unknown. John Oxley Library, State Library of Queensland Neg: 31364)*

We know little of Eliza before fate tossed her to the wild seas. She herself was elusive about her origins. We know she was born Eliza Ann Slack but it is not clear where. There are connections to Derbyshire and to Ceylon, as Sri Lanka was then known. Her year of birth is thought to have been 1798. When she married Captain Fraser she was twenty-one years old, and twenty years his junior. The marriage provided Eliza with a husband and a new home in Stromness in the Orkney Islands.

The Orkneys, a cluster of seventy islands ten kilometres from the north-eastern tip of the Scottish mainland, are a long way from Derbyshire and a world away from Ceylon. The islands have a stark beauty with their dramatic cliffs, smallish dark-brown houses, low-lying fertile green fields and heather moorland. The weather is unrelentingly windy, as the islands are exposed to both the Atlantic Ocean and the North Sea. Stromness was an active trading port when Eliza arrived, bustling with its fishing and whaling industries but also with a thriving farming sector. The isolated but resilient communities that lived there were deeply religious, with a strong and strict adherence to the Protestant scriptures, and it is easy to imagine that many a free-spirited woman felt suffocated in the tight-knit, pious community.

Eliza first told of surviving the shipwreck, the death of her husband, her capture by the 'cannibals' and her eventual rescue in *Narrative of the Capture, Sufferings, and Miraculous Escape of Mrs. Eliza Fraser*, which was published in 1837. The following year, a contemporary of hers, journalist and court reporter John Curtis, published another account, *Shipwreck of the Stirling Castle*. Curtis was very sympathetic to Eliza and her plight. But his style of telling the story, where Eliza is portrayed as a vulnerable white woman who finds herself among villainous black people, was not only left to that era. A similar tone and style can be found in Charles Barrett's *White Blackfellows: The Strange Adventures of Europeans Who Lived among Savages*, published in 1948, and Michael Alexander's *Mrs. Fraser on the Fatal Shore*, first published in 1971.

Although these accounts may not yield consistent historical fact, together they reveal much about colonial storytelling. Drawing on these sources, what follows is a constructed version of Eliza's tale that conveys the style and tone of the classic colonial captivity narrative.

The frontispiece and title page (overleaf) to *Shipwreck of the Stirling Castle* promise a tale of sensational drama. *(Artist unknown. John Oxley Library, State Library of Queensland Neg: 31365)*

SHIPWRECK

OF THE

STIRLING CASTLE,

CONTAINING

A FAITHFUL NARRATIVE OF THE DREADFUL SUFFERINGS OF THE CREW,

AND THE

CRUEL MURDER OF CAPTAIN FRASER

BY THE SAVAGES.

ALSO,

THE HORRIBLE BARBARITY OF THE CANNIBALS INFLICTED UPON

THE CAPTAIN'S WIDOW,

WHOSE UNPARALLELED SUFFERINGS ARE STATED BY HERSELF, AND
CORROBORATED BY THE OTHER SURVIVORS.

TO WHICH IS ADDED,

THE NARRATIVE OF THE WRECK OF THE

CHARLES EATON,

IN THE SAME LATITUDE.

Embellished with Engravings, Portraits, and Scenes illustrative of the Narrative.

BY JOHN CURTIS.

LONDON:

PUBLISHED BY GEORGE VIRTUE, IVY LANE,

AND SOLD BY ALL BOOKSELLERS.

M.DCCC.XXXVIII.

Eliza Fraser was a virtuous English gentlewoman, dutiful wife and mother – her three children remained at her home in the Orkney Islands under the care of the local Presbyterian minister while she accompanied her husband on his voyage. Curtis describes her as the ideal woman of her social standing:

> ... one, who being influenced by conjugal fidelity, and anxiety for the health and welfare of her husband, had left her country, children and friends, to console him in the hour of sickness and exhaustion ... performing the duties which the law of connubiality enjoins ...

Curtis also writes of

> ... The horrible barbarity of the Cannibals, inflicted upon THE CAPTAIN'S WIDOW, whose unparalleled sufferings are stated by herself ...

In the accounts of her tale, not much is made about the shipwreck itself – for it is only the beginning of her ordeal. After the *Stirling Castle* is lost, the crew launch two small boats – a longboat and a pinnace – and head south, hoping to reach the penal colony at Moreton Bay.

Captain Fraser, fifty-six years old and, according to the historical accounts, long afflicted with ill health, is in the longboat with Eliza and nine crew members, including the First Officer, Charles Brown. There are seven in the pinnace. Most of the supplies they salvage from the sinking boat are consumed in the first week, with only brandy and beer lasting longer.

The Captain is reluctant to land the boat because, like most seafarers of his time, he fears native violence and what he assumes will be their cannibalistic practices.

But, after floating for over a month, his crew, hungry and thirsty, are desperate to pull ashore to find some food and water. According to Curtis,

Despair and dismay sat upon every countenance, and they solemnly deliberated as to what should be done; and the only alternatives were to draw lots as to who should be sacrificed to supply food for the rest, or beach the boat, and all rush into eternity by one fell swoop! What an awful dilemma – our blood chills at the bare consideration of such unmitigated suffering.

Some accounts say that, while afloat, Eliza gives birth to a child who dies within a few minutes and is buried at sea. Although this is not referred to in Eliza's personal account, an editorial note appears at the end of her story, explaining that this omission is due to her natural reluctance to refer to the incident:

There be one important fact relating to the extreme sufferings of Mrs. Fraser, which, probably through

modesty she has failed to mention in her narrative …
Mrs. Fraser was delivered of a child, while up to her
waist in water in the long boat – the infant was
born alive but after a few gasps was drowned …

The longboat reaches the shore in July 1836. Upon arrival on dry land, contact with the Aborigines is at first tentative, laced with the fear and suspicion held by the Captain, his wife and the crew. Eliza describes the island's inhabitants as

… a band of frightful looking savages approaching
us, apparently with the ferocity of wild beasts …

According to Barrett,

On the third day after their landing, a regular system
of barter with the natives commenced.

The local Aboriginal people become less accommodating the longer the shipwrecked group stay on. Not until the crew have been at their makeshift camp for almost a fortnight do tensions increase between the newcomers and the traditional owners. Barrett says:

There was no trouble until the eleventh day, when
few articles of clothing remained, to exchange food.
The blacks were becoming hostile, and the outlook
was so grim …

Eventually, the Aboriginal people confront the party. They lead the shipwrecked men away, leaving Eliza alone on the beach. Eliza becomes a terrified 'prisoner' of the females of the tribe and is taken to her 'captors'' camp. She writes:

… I was visited by a very great number of their squaws, accompanied by their children, who first commenced with a close examination of my person, then to beating and maiming me with clubs, and, at the same time encouraging their children to follow their example, to pinch me, to pull my hair and to throw dirt into my face and eyes …

And:

When they had become weary of thus tormenting me, they put into my arms one of the most deformed, and ugly looking brats, that my eyes ever beheld; and then by signs gave me to understand that I must follow them …

In what Eliza sees as the ultimate insult, the Aboriginal women cover her sunburnt body with salt, charcoal and grease. This torture humiliates and demeans her, representing the cruelty that her captors are capable of inflicting upon her. As Alexander puts it:

… the prouder her posture, the more they seemed to be trying to humiliate her, slapping her with sticks and mimicking her walk with wicked parody.

The *Stirling Castle* had set sail from Hobart to Singapore on its fateful voyage. On the way out of the harbour, it hit another ship, an event that might well have been taken as a bad sign by the seventeen-member crew. Captain Fraser had a less than stellar record. He had lost a ship in the Torres Strait in 1830 and had damaged the *Stirling Castle* in 1835. The crew must have been full of gossip about his bad moods and poor judgement.

Despite surviving the shipwreck on the Swain Reefs, Captain Fraser perishes soon after he is taken into the Aboriginals' camp. According to Curtis he is a 'marked man' from the time he has contact with the Aboriginal people. The source of this tension is his determination to protect his wife.

The actual circumstances of Captain Fraser's death are unclear and the accounts vary. Some attribute his death to his pre-existing health problems; others claim that he was murdered, speared to death by his captors.

Barrett records the incident in his version of events:

> *Mrs. Fraser then hid behind a big tree. She went in fear of her black masters whose anger was easily aroused. And those now approaching were much excited and out of temper with each other, having perhaps been unsuccessful on a fishing expedition. Soon they walked away, all but three or four, who came towards the Captain. They suddenly stopped,*

> *when one of the party poised his spear, which he hurled at Captain Fraser, and the deadly weapon struck him near the shoulder-blade, and passing through his body, came out at his breast. Mrs. Fraser then darted from her hiding place ... With the boldness of a frantic woman, she ran and drew the accursed weapon from her dying husband ...*

In certain accounts of her experience, Eliza witnesses her husband's death. In others it occurs after she is taken to the female camps.

Later, during an inquiry in England into the shipwreck, Eliza gives evidence that she believes the death of her husband was accidental. Regardless of the circumstances,

This engraving from *Shipwreck of the Stirling Castle* depicts Captain Fraser's spearing. Opinions are divided, however, as to the actual cause of his death. *(Artist unknown. John Oxley Library, State Library of Queensland Neg: 107319)*

his death would have been distressing and heightened Eliza's sense of isolation and vulnerability in this strange land.

There is no doubt that the cultural practices of the Aboriginal people and the environment that Eliza is thrown into are alien to her. Little in her past would have prepared her for the experience of being stranded on a remote island with a tribe of Aboriginals. Eliza is horrified by their appearance and disgusted by their habits:

> *They were extremely filthy, never cleansing them-selves with water, and almost all, without scarcely an exception, were covered in vermin ...*

> *... their habitations but miserable hovels, fit only for those whose customs and habits degrade them to the level of young beasts ...*

In Eliza's story, the Aboriginal women are described as worse in their conduct, uglier in their appearance and more lacking in compassion for her than the men.

> *... I was sure to receive a sharp reprimand and sometimes a severe beating from my squaw-mistress ... Great was the abuse I received from this savage monster, who, in her fits of rage, would, beast-like, gnash her teeth, and sometimes seize me by the throat until I became nearly strangled ...*

This antagonism towards her is thought to be caused by the Aboriginal women's jealousy of their captive. Eliza, as a white woman, is assumed to be naturally more desirable to the Aboriginal men and so the women torment and demean her.

> *Her husband was the least savage of the two, apparently disposed to treat me with more humanity, but was evidently governed by his squaw, and dared to do nothing to cause her displeasure ...*

Eliza is expected to perform menial tasks – fetching water, watching babies, pounding grass seed, tending fires, and digging for roots and yams. She resents the chores she is forced to do and compares her state with that of slavery, which is all the crueller because of Eliza's supposed racial and cultural superiority to her captors. Alexander points out that

> *... though all the women were in a sense slaves, Mrs. Fraser was a slave to slaves. The women intensified their cruel treatment, whether through resentment, jealousy or natural predilection.*

In fact, as the Aboriginal people's natural superior, Eliza is seen as a potential catalyst for their civilisation through teaching them Christian ways and domestic skills. Michael Alexander gives the clearest account of the role a gentlewoman like Eliza could play in educating the savages with whom she is stranded. However, the Aboriginal women, in their primitive ignorance, fail to appreciate the opportunity Eliza's presence offers:

> *Mrs. Fraser would no doubt have been in her element and given selfless service to those less fortunate than she. The ladies of the tribe could have been taught needlework and hygiene and methods of cookery other than their endless broiling. Instruction in the English language might have followed and Sunday School to teach simple scripture been established. But in her present position her status as a superior being did not seem to be in any way appreciated.*

Eliza's captors move from campsite to campsite. This is tiring for Eliza, who is not used to such hard labour and physical exertion:

> *… I became so much exhausted as to be obliged to drop my burden, and by signs represent to my mistress that I could proceed no further; upon which she became, as usual, greatly enraged, and seizing me by the throat, commenced beating me, and continued to do so with so much violence that it would probably very soon have put a period to my existence, had not, her husband's brother humanely interposed on my behalf!*

Eliza's femininity gives her particular vulnerability and creates the spectre of sexual danger. This only escalates after her husband dies.

... my surprise, as well as disgust, to be visited by one of the most ugly and frightful looking Indians that my eyes ever beheld or that the whole island probably contained; with proposals that, 'as I had lost my mate, I should become his squaw!' Having made every sign possible of significant detestation and abhorrence in which he was held by me, and that death at his hands would be far preferable to my becoming his companion or 'squaw' ... I must (he represented to me) either voluntarily become his 'mate' or become so by compulsion! ... I was now placed in a situation more horrid than I had ever any previous conception of! Yea, even so much so as to be compelled to decide, and that too immediately, whether to become the willing companion and associate of a wild barbarous savage, or voluntarily suffer myself to become the defenceless victim of brutal outrage!

'... death at his hands would be far preferable to my becoming his companion or "squaw" ...'

Three surviving crew members of the shipwrecked *Stirling Castle* reach Moreton Bay on 8 August and sound the alarm. A search party is sent to rescue Eliza.

The rescuers arrive at Fig Tree Point, now part of the Great Sandy National Park on mainland Queensland, just in time. Eliza is about to be dragged off by one of the men, usually described as a 'chief'.

> *… without further ceremony or delay, [he] seized me by the shoulder, and fiend-like forced me within the enclosure of his dismal and filthy cabin …*

> *… but before he could accomplish his designs the God of mercy interposed, and sent one, as if commissioned expressly for the purpose, from Heaven, to rescue me, not from the devouring jaws of a ravenous lion, but from the hands of a savage ruffian, far more to be dreaded!*

Eliza describes her relief as the rescue party arrives:

> *… they arrived in season to frustrate the designs of the savage brute, who had selected me as his victim, and to rescue me from one of the most alarming situations in which an unfortunate female could be placed! I at that instant was held fast by the savage a few paces from the hut, but was discovered by Mr. Graham, who was a short distance ahead of the others, and was attracted to the thicket by my moans and entreaties for mercy!*

... he caught me in his arms, and hurried me to the boat ...

Most narrators attribute Eliza's rescue to the convict John Graham, who had a colourful history. On his arrival at the Sydney Cove penal colony, Graham was assigned to John Raine, a businessman at Parramatta, but was charged with petty larceny and sentenced to seven years at Moreton Bay.

He escaped and for six years lived with nearby Aboriginal clans, preferring this existence to life in the penal colony. Graham returned to Moreton Bay when he believed that his sentence was up, only to find that in his absence the colonial laws had changed and he was still

Another engraving in John Curtis's *Shipwreck of the Stirling Castle* imagines Eliza's 'rescue' from the Butchulla people. *(Artist unknown. John Oxley Library, State Library of Queensland Neg: 31363)*

required to serve his time. The authorities, however, were lenient with him because he had brought back valuable information about areas still unexplored by the colonial government.

It is this knowledge Graham employs when leading a party to rescue Eliza. According to this version of the story, he arrives at the camp just as Eliza is being dragged into a tent, presumably to suffer a 'fate worse than death'. Claiming Eliza as the ghost of his Aboriginal wife, Graham procures her release into his care, and takes her to where the rest of the party awaits.

He describes the moment of rescue:

Black and savage as they were, no horror struck me so much as the sight of that unhappy Lady, who caught my eye as it wandered round their Huts. Could I have armed myself with vengeance would I have been detained from giving the Cannibal race any account of my demands? Courage flushed to me and I feared no fate.

But Graham is not the only one credited with Eliza's rescue.

David 'Wandi' Bracefell is another escaped convict living among the Aboriginal people at this time. According to his claims, he befriends Eliza and helps her to escape but as soon as she reaches 'civilisation' she betrays him, threatening to make complaints about his behaviour towards her. The implication in this version of events is that Eliza has formed some kind of relationship with

Bracefell that she later regrets or is too embarrassed to admit to and, for this reason, she wishes to keep it concealed.

This account, with its theme of Eve's betrayal of Adam in the Garden of Eden, convinced some (notably male) writers recounting her tale over a century after the events. Barrett is sympathetic to Bracefell's account:

> *It is not impossible that he may even have brought her to the outskirts of Moreton Bay as he claimed, before a quarrel had caused him to abandon her to recapture by the blacks. A less fanciful supposition is that Graham was helped by Bracefell in the rescue operation.*

He adds:

> *If indeed Bracefell spoke truthfully, then Mrs. Fraser's suffering among savages had made her inhuman – a monster of ingratitude.*

Eliza arrives in Moreton Bay on 22 August, having spent fifty-two days with the Aboriginal people.

> *For some days after my deliverance, I felt the species of mental derangement which adverse fortune frequently produce; my mind was in continual agitation, and*

when at night I lost myself in sleep, I frequently awoke, thinking myself still in the power of the savages, whose terrific yells I imagined I distinctly heard! And at this moment, while writing and recalling to memory the dreadful scenes to which I have been witness, they present themselves to my imagination like a frightful dream!

She then sails to Sydney where she is received with generosity and sympathy; clothes are donated and funds raised for her return to her children in the Orkney Islands.

On the voyage back to England, Eliza marries the ship's Captain, Alexander Greene, just over five months after the death of her husband. She lands in Liverpool and applies to Police Commissioner Dowling for money to go to London.

In London she applies for more funds, presenting herself at Whitehall, where she requests an interview with the Secretary of State for the Colonies, Lord Glenelg. Still calling herself Mrs Fraser, she portrays herself as a poor widowed woman without means of support. She gives further interviews to the press, telling her story of capture by 'cannibals', describing their cruelty and barbarity, including the murder of her husband. As the details become more embellished, some begin to doubt her credibility.

Alexander addresses this:

Among other singularities she said that the barbarians had large tufts of blue hair growing upon their shoulders in the form of epaulets, and that their heads were quite denuded of hair, with the exception of the crown of the head from which streamed a large portion of the same texture and colour as the material forming their shoulder ornaments ... Mr. Dowling's confidence in her veracity immediately underwent a considerable diminution, and ordering her contemplated relief to be suspended for some time, he sent for the captain of the vessel in which she arrived from Sydney.

Public sympathy for Eliza is further strained when it becomes known that she has remarried and has concealed this during her first application for relief.

The Lord Mayor agrees to set up a committee to inquire into her situation. In light of the scandal over her marriage to Captain Greene, the Lord Mayor determines that the bulk of the money received should go to Captain Fraser's children rather than to Eliza. Others, including John Curtis, continue to vigorously defend Eliza.

Here was Mrs. Fraser, a virtuous woman, struggling with adversity, who left all to journey, with the man with whom she lived in connubial felicity for eighteen years, to the most distant part of another hemisphere, regardless alike of danger and death ... Supposing Mrs. Fraser had given a decided negative to [Greene's proposal], and she had sailed a five months' voyage as a 'companion', instead of a 'wife' – what then? Her virtue would doubtless have been preserved, (for virtuous who can doubt her to have been?) but her reputation probably might not; for even then, superficial readers, depreciating gossips (men as well as women) would have robbed her of her fair fame; and all these, too, emanating from persons who knew nothing of her, and never took the trouble to consider the precarious situation in which she stood … She has, we admit, acted foolishly in concealing a fact; but that ought to be construed in the most favourable terms.

Varying accounts exist of the fate of the rest of the crew – some drown (including the Captain's nephew), one is accidentally burned to death while asleep in a hut, two are left on a nearby island after a dispute with Aborigines, and one dies of exhaustion trying to get back to a settlement.

Only one survivor of the second boat to escape from the wrecked *Stirling Castle*, Robert Darge, makes it back to Sydney. Another survivor, Harry Youlden, publishes his version of events almost twenty years later. He paints an unflattering picture of a weak captain unable to assert control over his own crew and regards Eliza as a she-devil, referring to her as 'the most profane, artful, wicked woman that ever lived'. Youlden not only challenges other portrayals of Eliza Fraser's character but also gives a conflicting account of the attitude and behaviour of the Aboriginal people, saying that he and his companion were offered food and that the locals seemed concerned about their welfare.

It is noteworthy that while many from the *Stirling Castle* perish, Eliza survives. For all the portrayals of her as delicate, she must have had a strong constitution and a staunch will.

Eliza seems to have remained married to Captain Greene. They eventually migrate to New Zealand but, ironically, she dies in Australia in 1858 – in a carriage accident in Melbourne – aged sixty.

3

Methods and Motives

THE SAND GLOWS pink on Fraser Island as the sun sets on the beaches that face the Queensland mainland. The light is romantic and it is easy to see why people honeymoon here. I find the wilder, eastern side of the island – particularly around Orchid Beach, where Eliza and her fellow shipwreck survivors landed – more spectacular, but here on the western side there is a welcoming calm.

Relaxing and taking in the changing light after a day of swimming, fishing and four-wheel-driving, one would think this land a paradise born of another world. But it is not so hard to imagine that this natural wonderland could seem like a hell on earth to Eliza. In a landscape so foreign to her, she'd be uncertain as to whether she would make it back to her own kind, and bewildered by the strange ways of the Aboriginal people. It is easy to understand her fear.

Eliza's story is a simple one: a woman is shipwrecked, her husband dies and she must survive among a 'primitive' tribe in order to find her way back to civilisation – and to safety – or at least survive long enough to be rescued. In order for this simple story to work as a gripping tale, however, several elements need to be in place. Eliza has to be very good; the Aboriginal people have to be very bad. They need to be barbaric and violent – indeed, they are portrayed as cannibals – to increase the danger that Eliza is in, to heighten the drama. The story isn't as compelling if Eliza finds herself among friendly natives or kind Aboriginals. Where is the suspense in that? And where is the thrill or heroics in rescuing Eliza if she isn't really in any danger? No-one would pay to see that movie.

> *… where is the thrill or heroics in rescuing Eliza if she isn't really in any danger?*

Each step taken to enhance these dramatic elements of the story is a step away from the reality of what actually happened. Breaking the elements down gives an understanding of how the story is told to achieve the most dramatic effect. And, when *how* the story is told is clear, investigating *why* it is told becomes easier.

ELIZA: THE PURE AND GOOD

I think of the portrait of Eliza Fraser with the shawl modestly wrapped around her shoulders as I read descriptions of her in the various accounts of her story.

Eliza is a virtuous, moral woman from a middle-class background but the story, especially as told by others, treats her as a symbol of something more. She becomes the embodiment of all that is right and proper about the Empire; she is the epitome of Britannia. Eliza's capture is a metaphor for the danger that 'non-whites' pose to white society, especially in the untamed colonies. This concept of the British Empire could only be projected onto the most moral of women. Convict or working-class women, for example, could never embody this image in the same way. In Eliza's case, her vulnerability, innocence and chastity are highlighted, and her reputation is defended when insinuations of fraud arise.

Sarah Carter, in her book *Capturing Women*, explains how white women were portrayed in colonial literature as objects of purity, symbols of domesticity, and that they were viewed as the moral standard-bearers of their race – and class – with a duty to exert moral influence, as wives and mothers, over men. This moral pedestal is the kind described by philosopher Jean-Jacques Rousseau in *Émile* when he writes that 'public opinion is the tomb of a man's virtue and the throne of a woman's' and that women's honour 'does not rest on their conduct but on their reputation'.

But Eliza's pedestal is also a gilded cage. Her story is taken and told by male narrators like John Curtis, and in their hands she becomes a valuable but defenceless object to be rescued in a heroic tale. Eliza and her purity, modesty and virtue become the prize in a boys'-own-adventure version of her rescue. On the colonial frontier, where there are few white women, Eliza is precious, exotic and rare.

While Eliza's story may elevate the white woman as a symbol, it is also a way of subordinating Eliza herself as a person. It is this characterisation of vulnerability and innocence of women that kept them in the home, under the control and supervision of fathers and husbands who claimed that women needed protection and lacked the capacity for independence. Under nineteenth-century British law, women were chattels of their husbands, unable to vote and prevented from owning and inheriting property.

To make Eliza appear purer and more chaste, more genteel, more civilised, her virtues are contrasted against the character of the natives, who are depicted as being menacing and dangerous, savage and cannibalistic. They are not merely different from her; they are a threat to her.

Of course, the real Eliza must have been far from a helpless damsel in distress. She has a tenacious will to survive and makes it safely home when many of her male companions perish. And indeed, as Eliza discovers, public sympathy for her evaporates once people learn that she has remarried and now, with her new husband, has a new protector. No wonder she keeps her marriage secret.

ABORIGINAL PEOPLE: BASE AND BRUTAL

Throughout the Eliza Fraser narratives, the superiority of whites is asserted. In his descriptions of Aboriginal people, John Curtis refers to their animalistic traits and their lowly status on the evolutionary ladder. Here are selected samples of his opinions that these days many people would find very offensive:

This was certainly a prudent precaution, but they afterwards learned that it was a useless one, for such is the sensitiveness of the olfactory nerve of these barbarians, that they can scent the progress of Europeans as well as their quadruped brethren, the bloodhounds …

Many of both sexes, when young, are far from ugly; nay, some of them are tolerably handsome, but the old women are absolute frights, and appear only to want an additional member to render them analogous with the long-tailed fraternity …

Having no impelling motive to the performance of a good action, and nothing to deter them from a bad one, no wonder that they are sunk so low in the thermometer, and almost to the very zero, of civilization …

It would really seem that these untutored brutes had been well instructed in the art of teasing; and they strongly remind us of the pranks of a domestic animal of the feline species, who delights in torturing her helpless victims before she devours them …

These demons in human form employed every method which they could devise, to torture and annoy their miserable captives.

By portraying white people as superior, good and civilised, and blacks as inferior, bad and uncivilised, most versions of Eliza's story set up a clear 'us' and 'them' dichotomy. The differences between the two races run deep – as distinct as night and day, black and white.

To further emphasise the superiority of the 'civilised' whites, and the savagery of the blacks, the latter's purported barbaric practices are also highlighted. In the 1937 publication *John Graham, Convict, 1824*, a fictionalised account of Graham's rescue story, author and artist Robert Gibbings provides the following description of Aboriginal people dancing:

With their feet far apart and every muscle of their legs twitching so that the whole body seemed to tremble they would dance back-to-back, suddenly twisting about and facing each other, then as suddenly turning again and continuing their wild orgy of quivering flesh.

Such descriptions of these 'barbaric practices' reinforced notions of the inherently savage nature of the people themselves, while little was done to clarify the observations made by Eliza Fraser about Aboriginal culture. Eliza's accounts are full of claims of savagery and bloodlust to an extent that seems incredible. Curtis provides many examples in his text:

> *In common with all savages, revenge with them is never satiated till quenched in the blood of an adversary. Like the Chinese, they are not particular about the person; but if a <u>white</u> injures or offends them, they generally satisfy their rage upon the first of that colour they can conveniently meet with. In their wild state they know not what it is either to <u>forget or forgive</u>; and when once they murder a white, always expect retaliation for it, whatever appearance of friendship the other whites may put on, believing that they are yet to suffer, and that only fear or the want of an opportunity prevents a reprisal; hence, until some of the tribe are killed by whites, they never consider themselves safe, and <u>they usually continue their murderings until, in retaliation, blood is expiated in blood</u>.*

ABORIGINAL MEN: LECHEROUS AND DANGEROUS

A front plate in Gibbings's book starkly illustrates this aspect of the narrative. As Aboriginal women dance, a white figure hides her face in shame, her arms used to hide her modestly, in contrast to the nakedness that the Aboriginal women revel in. In the background, an older Aboriginal man looms, leering at Eliza. The white woman's sexuality is seen as being lecherously desired and prized by Aboriginal men. Gibbings describes it this way:

> *But even in primitive society the exotic has its charm, and many a night as she lay under her covering of bark, dark forms would slink around and lusting faces would try to lure her from the camp.*

Eliza's sexual peril is the titillating undercurrent in her story and an important source of dramatic tension.

Frontispiece woodcut by Robert Gibbings in his book *John Graham, Convict, 1824. (Courtesy of the Estate of Robert Gibbings and the Heather Chalcroft Literary Agency)*

Although Eliza does not meet the 'fate worse than death' during her 'captivity', in her story the danger is always there, lurking at every turn. Her situation taps into broader fears that were prevalent at the time of her ordeal. The threat of miscegenation, of diluting the purity of the white race, especially by black men, was always feared. Eliza's predicament is a situation ripe with that danger, as personified in a libidinous black man.

Captivity narratives like Eliza's often allude to the mistreatment of Aboriginal women within their own communities; they are referred to as 'beasts of burden' and other descriptions that imply a subordinate and subservient position to Aboriginal men. Such narratives work to further exaggerate the savagery of the Aboriginal men. This demonising of Aboriginal men is generally done without any irony or reflection on the subordinate and subservient place of women in European society at the time.

Patrick White's novel *A Fringe of Leaves* was inspired by Eliza Fraser's story but in several ways digresses from the classic captivity narrative. White can always be relied on to explore the complexities and hypocrisy inherent in a society's class system. In the case of this novel he investigates these themes through a working-class heroine elevated in social status by marriage. This allows him to cleverly compare the drudgery faced by women from England's working and poorer classes with the labour required of women in a hunter-gatherer society.

ABORIGINAL WOMEN: MEAN AND JEALOUS

Just as white women reflect the moral standards of their community in frontier stories, Aboriginal women play the same role for theirs. With this role as standard-bearer for their race, it is not surprising that Aboriginal women in these tales are never portrayed as morally good. Instead, they are used as symbols of the degeneracy and savagery attributed to their race by white authors. While white femininity is equated with virtue, domestication and positive moral influences, Aboriginal women are portrayed as the antithesis of idealised womanhood.

In Eliza's tale, Aboriginal women are described as even more treacherous than black men. They are portrayed as being pettier and meaner, and having less sympathy for Eliza's plight than the men do. They are made to seem physically threatening and dangerous, without domestic skill or maternal instinct.

Sidney Nolan
Mrs Fraser 1947
Ripolin enamel on hardboard
66.2 x 107 cm
Purchased 1995 with a special allocation from the Queensland Government. Celebrating the
Queensland Art Gallery's Centenary 1895–1995
Collection: Queensland Art Gallery
Reproduced with the permission of the Trustees of the Sidney Nolan Trust/Bridgeman Art Library

Sidney Nolan became intrigued with the story of Eliza Fraser when he visited Fraser Island. He was
particularly fascinated by the version of the story in which Eliza, while living among the Aboriginal
people, becomes romantically involved with the escaped convict David Bracefell, whom she betrays
upon her rescue. There seems to be something intriguing about the notion that, in the natural environment, all the trappings and confines of class and culture can be stripped away and what we are
left with is our most primal, natural and instinctive self. It is this concept that Nolan captures in the
portrait that he commenced work on during his stay on the island. The end result highlights Eliza's
desperation and degradation, but it also melds her into the landscape.

It is impossible to know all the facts about Eliza Fraser's circumstances. They have been lost long ago and even the personal testimonies of survivors and Eliza herself are steeped in contradictions about what actually happened. But in some ways the facts are not the most interesting thing about Eliza's story and its iconic place in Australian folklore.

This woman's story might have been a simple one, but it would come to be used for many complex purposes – well beyond anything that Eliza herself might have imagined. Eliza had her own motivations for the embellishment of her experiences. But there are other reasons why the story has been told the way it has, factors enhancing its appeal and serving specific purposes. The tale of civilisation versus savagery, of white against black, of 'us' and 'them' reveals much about the prevailing values and ideologies of Eliza's time.

GAINING MONEY OR PARDON

Eliza Fraser was no doubt traumatised by her experience but upon rescue she began to exaggerate her tale. By the time she arrived back in Sydney what happened to her was already being sensationalised in the newspapers. Reports of Eliza's story began to differ from her original account. This continued in London, where pecuniary reward encouraged her emphasis on savagery, cruelty and

Like the text within, the frontispiece to *Narrative of the Capture, Sufferings, and Miraculous Escape of Mrs. Eliza Fraser* likens the Butchulla people to Native Americans. *(Artist unknown. Courtesy of the National Library of Australia)*

torture. The more sympathy she could garner, the more donations she received.

Accounts of Eliza's captivity were also altered, often dramatically, depending on the intended readership. In North America, stories about the capture of white women by Indians had become a lucrative business, and Eliza tailored her tale accordingly. This commercial agenda can be seen in the terminology she uses: 'chiefs', 'wigwams' and 'squaws' are referred to in some versions of the story.

Eliza would go on to demonise the 'natives' and exaggerate their savagery, peddling her story for her own advantage. But, although this was a cruel thing to do to the Aboriginal people who had ensured her survival, I don't judge her for this approach. We don't know much about her circumstances once she returned to London, and she may well have had to be enterprising to ensure her own economic security – as well as that of her children. Women in her time didn't often have a lot of choices. And I don't criticise her for being entrepreneurial if that was the case. Eliza's resilience in the strange environs of Fraser Island shows that she was a resourceful woman, a survivor.

But Eliza was not the only person who told her story and nor was she the only one who had something to gain from its embellishment.

John Graham's pardon rested on his bravery in rescuing Eliza. This was his inducement for exaggerating the danger that she was in and, in turn, the barbarity of the Aboriginal people she was supposedly held captive by. His own account is reproduced in Michael Alexander's book:

> *That John Graham here was forced to venture every thing by himselfe not only to Save the lives of the unhappy people they had carried away ... That on The 7th of August 1836, he freed Mrs. Fraser from seven hundred Canniballs and savages ... he succeeded to take her from thoes frightful Clans – and hoards of Canniballs and savages and carried her upwards of 40 miles with the assistance of 4 blacks that came with him from the mountains ... and thus by himselfe risqued all and freed all ... That his Superior knowledge of the country and*

Language kept them all from harm and even the Savage from being killed after all Thoes promises I am still detained and after venturing my life to save and face the waves in open boats after Delivering four Christians from the Canniballs and savage what no other person would do I hope to be rewarded.

Graham had, by this time, lived with the Aboriginal people throughout the area for many years, preferring their company and culture to that of his own people who had settled in Moreton Bay. It was his knowledge of their culture and his relationship with them that assisted him in locating Eliza. He would have known that they were not cannibals. He would have understood the dynamics of their community. But this would not have served the purpose of creating a narrative where he was instrumental in rescuing Eliza from peril, especially the expected 'fate worse than death'. Graham was after a pardon, and a story of friendly natives in which Eliza is cared for – even if she had trouble fitting in – would not have created the heroism needed to secure his long-desired goal. Graham's tactics worked. He was eventually granted a ticket-of-leave and £10 for his efforts.

SAVING SOULS AND CIVILISING SAVAGERY

In some accounts it is not the Aboriginals of Fraser Island who save Eliza from the shipwreck but God who saves her from the natives. And it is her unwavering belief in

Him and His teaching that leads to Eliza's survival and safe return to civilisation. Curtis writes:

We ardently hope that all those who have been especial objects of favour in the sight of Heaven, so as to escape from their enemies by miracle, will ever evince their gratitude to Him who hath brought them out of 'the valley of the shadow of death' – and they can only do so by keeping his commandments.

Given the predominant role that religion played in European culture at the time, Eliza Fraser's faith was not unusual. Curtis's version highlights the way in which Eliza's deliverance from the savages was used to reinforce religious beliefs, particularly as an example of how faith can assist in overcoming adversity and fear.

… it would be better to implore the forgiveness of God, and resign themselves quietly to their fate. What an awful moment of terror and dismay! – but their resolution was a wise one, for it is much safer to fall into the 'hands of God, than the hands of wicked and cruel men' …

Our history exhibits not only a detail of the barbarity of the heathen, but also the benevolence of the Christian; and moreover the splendid liberality of a generous public …

Eliza herself strikes this same chord:

> *… she unceasingly looked to and called upon Heaven for that help which it appeared not then in the power of any human being alone to afford her; and to be thus so suddenly and unexpectedly rescued from the power of one who was about to plunge her into a state of inconceivable wretchedness, must be admitted as proof positive that in whatever situation we may be placed, however forlorn and apparently hopeless our condition, we still have a friend, whom, if in Him we put our trust, we shall find both able and willing to stay the assassin's hand, even at the instant when raised to inflict the fatal blow!*

Curtis uses the event as proof of the need to bring Christianity to the 'savages' and he makes the strongest call for missionary zeal in converting them:

> *Before we commence our interesting narrative, we cannot refrain from indulging the hope that the perusal will act as a stimulus to missionary exertions, and that the various societies who have long engaged in sending persons to preach the gospel to those who 'sit in darkness and in the shadow of death;' we trust that a holy emulation will arise among them, who shall be the first to send a missionary to the shore where the natives inflict these unheard tortures.*

Yet another consequence of this story and its telling as a story of enlightenment over dark savagery is neatly summed up by Aboriginal historian Lynette Russell:

> *They wrote of an Australia populated with malicious violent savages whose salvation would be exchanged for access to the land.*

This missionary agenda worked alongside the dispossession and control of Aboriginal people, and in his account of Eliza's tale Curtis contemplates the broader agenda for colonisation that occurred at the time of the *Stirling Castle*'s shipwreck:

> *There appears to be a degree of force necessary to urge a man towards civilization in his primitive, debased state, and cause him to divest himself of the habits which he has acquired. It is only when the mind is more enlightened, and reason supersedes animal instinct, that civilization will speedily advance among the community, and this must be effected by the exertions of its individual members; nor can this be reasonably expected, without Divine interposition, to be the work of one generation ...*
>
> *Persons who have had an opportunity of obtaining some knowledge of these savages, are of opinion that very many lives might be saved if timely and efficient means were adopted; for it has been observed that when the various tribes of Australia have been fairly*

satisfied of their inferior power and strength to contest with the whites, they ever after show a disinclination for hostility.

The portrayal of Aboriginal people and their culture as savage does not only provide a clear justification of the Christianising mission. It also allows a broader narrative and purpose to play out. It is not just about saving Aboriginal souls; there is a desire to take their lands.

CAPTIVITY NARRATIVES AND THE FRONTIER

Images of white female vulnerability were exploited in nineteenth-century Australia to convey the necessity of policing Aboriginal communities. Sarah Carter makes this observation when considering how captivity narratives were used on the Canadian frontier:

It was important that white women were seen to be not only helpless but powerless, without a voice of their own, and to be the property of white men; thus, according to [sociologist Vron] Ware, 'their "protectors" could claim to be justified in taking revenge for any alleged insult or attack on them.'

This is precisely what happened with Eliza Fraser's story. Captivity narratives form a part of Australian frontier folklore, and they emerged at a time that has more significance than we might appreciate. The clear inferiority of Aboriginal people and the barbarism of their culture as portrayed in a story like Eliza Fraser's was relied on to justify their dispossession and to ignore their connections to their traditional country, their own laws and their own systems of decision-making.

These stories of native barbarity and the threat that they posed may seem quaint today, but they were particularly important at moments on the frontier when tensions arose between coloniser and colonised. At these points of conflict, stories like Eliza's, when told in this way, provided the justification for force, violence and dominance, and were used to gain support for plans to eradicate, subdue, tame, contain and control Aboriginal people.

Historian Kay Schaffer has written extensively on Eliza Fraser. In her book *In the Wake of First Contact: The Eliza Fraser Stories*, she notes the link between the popularity of Eliza's story and frontier conflict in the era in which Eliza was shipwrecked and held 'captive'. She observes that the Queensland settlement wars of the 1850s brought the Aboriginal people and the 'invading populations of settlers into closer contact and provoked more overt violence and savagery'. Writer Veronica Brady (also an authority on Patrick White), in an essay titled 'A Properly Appointed Humanism? *A Fringe of Leaves* and the Aborigines', also makes the link between Eliza Fraser's story and the frontier violence that followed as active dispossession of the island took place during the decades after she was shipwrecked. According to Brady, the tale was the 'excuse for at least two large-scale massacres of Aborigines in the nineteenth century'.

Eliza's story is imbued with British fears and insecurities about both the frontier and Aboriginal people. As the extracts from Curtis's book show, Eliza's story became a platform from which to denigrate and dehumanise the 'natives', and create negative assumptions and stereotypes about Aboriginal people as being culturally and biologically inferior.

Eliza's story is imbued with British fears and insecurities about both the frontier and Aboriginal people.

Once these anxieties found expression and form in narratives such as Eliza's, they justified the mechanisms for surveillance of Aboriginal people through policing practices, legal control and government policy. They allowed the law to overlook and sanction violence against the Indigenous population.

These narratives also allowed writers to transfer the violence of their own culture onto that of the Aborigines. They contain accounts of the brutish way of life of Aboriginal people but are curiously devoid of accounts of brutality within penal colonies or of violence against Aboriginal people. Eliza Fraser's story says: 'they' are the barbarians, not 'us'.

4

The Other Side of the Story

FRASER ISLAND IS the traditional land of the Butchulla people. They call this land K'gari. In Eliza Fraser's story, the Butchulla are an undifferentiated mass, anonymous entities employed to play the role of a hostile people who lead a savage life on an inhospitable land. They are never named in the text, either as a group or as individuals. They are as silent throughout the text as they are shadowy. They are the 'captors', 'savages' and 'cannibals'.

But the Butchulla have their own history, their own worldview and their own version of the time when the survivors of the shipwrecked *Stirling Castle* lived among them. Had she not been taken in by the Butchulla, Eliza most likely would have perished. The area was experiencing a severe drought when she landed on the island, and the crew's arrival would have put considerable pressure on already scarce resources; their separation into different camps was most likely an attempt by the Butchulla to share the burden created by the influx of outsiders who had arrived unexpectedly.

Some surviving crew members contradicted Eliza's claims of barbarity and cruelty, expressing admiration and gratitude towards the Aboriginal people who helped them to survive. One crew member, Robert Darge, could even place the fear the Aboriginal people had of white people in a proper context:

> *I don't think they would have killed me. But there were some who could not bear the sight of a white man at all. I believe that the reason they had such a hatred of me was that the soldiers wounded them.*

Darge also refuted the popular portrayals of cannibalism:

> *I do not believe that any of the tribes I was amongst ate human flesh. I never saw anything of the kind.*

In fact, Kay Schaffer has observed in her research that some crew members noted that the behaviour of the Aborigines was less hostile than the behaviour between some members of the destitute crew.

A BUTCHULLA PERSPECTIVE

Aboriginal Elder Olga Miller has given a rare and insightful perspective on the Eliza Fraser story. With her knowledge of oral history, Miller enlightens for the first time what Eliza's appearance might have meant from the perspective of a traditional owner. She explains the perplexing problem that Eliza Fraser posed upon her arrival.

> *The women were uncertain as to what to do with this white lubra, so the Clever Woman decided it was better to take her down to where the men were … The men were not at all pleased with the arrival of the women with the stranger … The women had marked the 'stranger' with 'ochre signs' which read 'let this woman through' and 'do not harm this woman'.*

Far from being the danger to Eliza, the Butchulla women were responsible for her safety; far from being jealous of her, they took responsibility for her survival.

> *I do not know if it has ever been recorded by European writers, but there was an instance spoken of by our local men of those days. It seems 'the stranger woman' did not realise that she had to help gather firewood as her contribution towards being fed. One man of the group who had joined Durrumboi's party pushed and shoved her angrily. In no time, he was impaled with several Badtjalla [Butchulla] spears. The signs the Badtjalla women had marked on her had to be obeyed.*

Miller says that when Eliza Fraser first arrived she was suffering from terrible sunburn as a result of being exposed to the elements during the weeks she was at sea in the longboat. When she came into the women's camp, the women covered her in salt, grease and charcoal to help the severe burns to heal and later to keep her warm. In her own story, Eliza mistook this as torture, an attempt to humiliate her and a sign of jealousy.

The Butchulla women also made a white ochre mark across Eliza's body, a sign that indicated to others that she had the protection of the women's camp and anyone who harmed her would have to answer to them. Rather than being her 'tormentors', these women were her protectors and made sure that she was in no danger of the 'fate worse than death'.

It appears that the lasting impression Eliza left on the Butchulla who helped her survive was that she was an ungrateful guest – one who betrayed their kindnesses. She was not capable of doing the simplest tasks asked of her and was indifferent to the valued principle of reciprocity. Moreover, according to Miller, the Butchulla were both angry and hurt at the way that Eliza had misrepresented them after she was rescued, though they also hypothesised that she had been affected by her ordeal.

> *... to us Mrs Fraser was never a very important person because we knew she was a big waterhole, and that means you're a big fibber ... they said she was 'brundy'. Brundy means 'not all there'. But she was affected by the sun, very sunburnt.*

Placing Miller's version beside Eliza's allows us to see the cultural conflict and a clash of values. It is also clear that the Butchulla side of the story was pushed aside and they were recast in the role of the villains as Eliza Fraser's story gained in popularity and became part of the colonial folklore.

Butchulla artist Fiona Foley has critiqued the Eliza Fraser captivity narrative in her work. She sees the depiction of her community in the story as a mirror that shows colonial Australia a reflection of itself. What the white intruders accused the Butchulla of being was what they knew themselves to be:

> *It is the omnipresent Aboriginal gaze which reflects your colonial gaze. What I see mirrored in the exclusive gaze of race is an inarticulate consumption of guilt, an awkward Australia.*

Foley has also observed that in photos Butchulla women are always nameless. She has parodied this in a series of self-portraits in which she models the traditional poses of Aboriginal women being photographed. In one, she wears a reed and shell necklace. In another, the handle of a hand-woven basket stretches across her forehead. By reclaiming these traditional images, Foley celebrates the continuation of the Butchulla culture and the resilience of the Butchulla women.

Fiona Foley
Badtjala Woman (with collecting bag) 1994
Photograph
45 x 35 cm

Native Blood (detail) 1994
Type C photograph
57 x 47.5 cm

(Courtesy of the artist and Niagara Galleries)

Eliza's captivity narrative helped to shape what was 'known' about Aboriginal people and their culture. People read stories about her and believed what was said about the barbarity of the people she encountered. Perhaps because these accounts contained so many generally accepted negative stereotypes of Aboriginal people – they were cannibals, they were cruel, they were lecherous, they were savage – readers simply saw her story as reinforcing what they already knew.

The stories about Eliza portray her arrival as a point of first contact, as though she were the first white person whom the Aborigines on the island had met. But there appear to have been several white men – mostly escaped convicts – who had long associations and complex relationships with Aboriginal people. There were already several white men living with the Butchulla when Eliza Fraser arrived.

For those convicts, Aboriginal life seemed far more desirable than colonial life, and there is some irony in the way in which convicts left behind the brutality and cruelty of the penal colonies to shelter with the 'brutal' and 'cruel' Aborigines. Their presence in the island communities shows another way in which the Butchulla offered protection to white people.

The Eliza Fraser story is premised on the danger that blacks posed to whites, especially white women. Aboriginal people were repeatedly portrayed as fierce, violent, sexually threatening and dangerous. This dominant and negative stereotype hid the reality of the dangers on the frontier and outright denied that it was the Aboriginal people who were much more vulnerable to any violence.

Frontier violence against Aboriginal people has been recounted in some sources in such a matter-of-fact manner that it was evidently not just commonplace but acceptable. To take one example, consider the unremarkable way it is alluded to in this extract from the autobiography of RM Williams, *I Once Met a Man*:

> *He was shepherding a long string of naked Aboriginals, all chained and hurrying to keep up with the camel he, Virgo, rode ... Far to the north there was an Aboriginal extermination programme going on. An old prospector called Brooks had been murdered and put down a rabbit burrow west of Alice Springs, and whole families of blacks had been shot in reprisals. Whites in the west carried hand guns in those days and used them ... The wild tribes were hostile and understandably so as they could still remember Giles and Warburton going through fifty years before.*

Kay Schaffer observes that historians have estimated that for every instance of violence by Aboriginal people, the settlers retaliated tenfold. In tracing the impact of colonisation on the Butchulla, she articulates a link between their fate and Eliza's story. According to Schaffer's research, when the *Stirling Castle* was shipwrecked in 1836 there were an estimated 2,000 to 3,000 people living on Fraser Island. By 1904, the remaining 218 Butchulla were sent to reserves or penal colonies on the mainland. The Butchulla were dispossessed of their land.

GENUINE FRONTIER CAPTIVITY STORIES

Eliza's story might have attracted great public interest, but in truth the number of 'white women captured by cannibals', of European women forced to live among the Aborigines, was few. Perhaps this is part of the mystique of Eliza's tale. The focus on her 'captivity' diverts attention from the most common frontier abduction and captivity narrative – that of Aboriginal women being abducted and sexually abused by white men on the frontier. Eliza's story replaces the more common story with an exceptional one.

> *Eliza's story replaces the more common story with an exceptional one.*

The story also covers up other experiences of Aboriginal women on the frontier. In the early days of colonisation, white women were dependent on the skills of Aboriginal women, especially in relation to childbirth and the care of infants. Anthropologist Nicolas Peterson estimates that Aboriginal women provided between 60 and 90 per cent

The treatment of Aboriginal people was often dehumanising. *(Artist unknown. State Library of Western Australia, 011287D)*

of the food in their communities, giving them considerable economic power. Because of this power they were not the drudges and slaves that they were portrayed as by (mostly male) anthropologists.

Another anthropologist, Fay Gale, notes a cultural and gender bias in these observations, claiming that until recently, the majority of writers about Aboriginal culture have been men who often assumed that Aboriginal men occupied the same dominant position in their community as men in Western society. These writers did not notice that Aboriginal women enjoyed a greater degree of economic independence than white women did.

Even contemporary accounts perpetuate this stereotype.

Robert Hughes, in his 1987 book, *The Fatal Shore*, while discussing the attitudes towards marriage of the Iora (Eora), the traditional owners of parts of Sydney, describes the view of Aboriginal women in the following way:

> *Both before and after [marriage], she was merely a root-grubbing, shell-gathering chattel, whose social assets were wiry arms, prehensile toes and a vagina.*

Outside observers like Hughes often failed to understand the social power that women's labour helped them to secure. Aboriginal societies were more complex than outsiders assumed, especially those from Western cultures in which women had little power, economic or otherwise.

The portrayal of Aboriginal women in colonial narratives like Eliza Fraser's story disempowered Aboriginal women by omitting any mention of the roles and power they had in their own community. Described as 'beasts of burden' and the chattels of Aboriginal men, they were placed at the lowest level of the colonial socio-economic hierarchy. This deprived Aboriginal women of the recognition of their authority, responsibility and independence.

At the same time, white women in colonial settings were portrayed as paragons of purity and a symbol of the Empire. By comparison, Aboriginal women were portrayed as bad mothers, inept providers, vindictive, uncaring and unloving. These depictions placed Indigenous women well outside the ideals of motherhood and femininity that the iconic white woman represented. Thus, it is perhaps no surprise that stories about the capture of Aboriginal women were ignored.

While there were many women abducted on the frontier, they were almost always Aboriginal women being abducted by non-Aboriginal men. It is the legacy of colonialism, and the result of any war, that the women of the conquered are assumed to become the property of the conquering; and with the scarcity of white women on the frontier, Aboriginal women were in demand for their sexual services and their labour.

Colonial stereotypes implied that Aboriginal women were 'available' as sexual partners or for prostitution, thereby negating accusations of rape and freeing white men from taking responsibility for their half-caste children. Rather than condemning the predatory sexual violence of white men, any so-called immorality on the frontier was blamed on the behaviour of Aboriginal women. They were portrayed as promiscuous and accustomed to being treated with contempt in their own society, and to being bought and sold as commodities by their husbands. Depicting Aboriginal women as lewd and licentious deflected attention away from the actions of white men, including the government officials supposedly in positions as protectors.

Historian Henry Reynolds writes in *Why Weren't We Told?*:

> *Mates shared black women with their fellows – and were expected to do so in a way that would not have*

happened with white women, other than prostitutes. Shared sex without affection and responsibility strengthened male bonding. Complicity in atrocity, abuse and abduction added greatly to the sense of solidarity.

In his book *The Explorers*, Tim Flannery reproduces an extract from the 1883 diary of Emily Creaghe:

20 February – … The usual method here of bringing in a new wild gin is to put a rope around her neck and drag her along from horseback, the gin on foot.

21 February – The new gin whom they call Bella is chained up to a tree a few yards from the house, and is not to be loosed until they think she is tamed.

Creaghe's matter-of-fact observation of the treatment of Aboriginal women and girls reveals how commonplace – and acceptable – this behaviour was. After they had been taken by force, Aboriginal women were sometimes kept in irons to prevent their escape until they were too terrified to make any attempt to return to their own families.

Ready access to black women was seen as one of the attractions of outback life, and women were forcibly abducted in all parts of Australia. Police officers reported that when men on stations saw 'lubras' in the bush they would pursue them, run them down on their horses and take them away. As Henry Reynolds records in *The Other Side of the Frontier*:

> *Torres Strait Islanders told a government official in 1882 that the white men had so ill-treated their women in the past that when a boat was sighted the young women were buried in the sand and kept there until the Europeans sailed away.*

A couple of decades later, in 1904, the Normanton Protector of Aborigines noted that it was common practice for Europeans to round up 'small mobs of wild natives' and sexually assault their women. Historian Ann McGrath in her book *Born in the Cattle* devotes a chapter to 'Black Velvet', a name given to Aboriginal women. She writes about carloads of men from bush townships and construction camps raiding the station camps for women. Tennant Creek police records from December 1935 detail an occasion when two white men visited the camp in a car with loaves of bread to exchange for women. When their demands were refused, they laid poison that killed twenty camp dogs. Other whites assaulted Aboriginal men who tried to protect Aboriginal women, evidence of the violence Aborigines had to tolerate when they refused to supply women for prostitution. It is clear from encounters such as these that Aboriginal women were likely to be taken forcibly if they were simply not 'handed over' to white men in search of sexual gratification.

Conflict over women was a constant feature of frontier

relations, and sexual relations between white men and black women were a major source of misunderstanding, bitterness and conflict. Under Aboriginal law, violation of Aboriginal women was usually met with severe punishment, but when this was meted out by blacks against white men who had violated Aboriginal women, it was met with violence from 'avenging' colonists.

In *Aborigines and Colonists: Aborigines and Colonial Society in New South Wales in the 1830s and 1840s*, historian RHW Reece writes that 'the trouble arose when the whites refused to supply the tea, sugar and other items which they had promised to the Aborigines in return for their women'. Hostility often arose from stockmen's interference with Aboriginal women, to the extent that in 1837 Governor Bourke recognised that the kidnapping of Aboriginal women was one of the main causes of conflict between Aborigines and whites. Bourke attempted, unsuccessfully, to prohibit whites from forcibly detaining Aboriginal women.

Being portrayed on the frontier as cheap or free sexual partners, and being known to accept small rewards for sexual favours, saw Aboriginal women labelled as 'low-class' prostitutes. This stereotype of easy sexual access meant that Aboriginal women had little protection from the colonial law when they suffered sexual abuse and exploitation, with allegations against white men usually dismissed.

The relationship between black women and white men on the frontier was complex. Some Aboriginal women were forced into relationships with white men; others were bartered and bargained for in brief economic exchanges – either on their own initiative or at their husband's behest – or were 'loaned' to white men on a more long-term basis in exchange for a supply of food to be provided to the woman's parents or her promised husband. And some Aboriginal women chose to enter into relationships with white men.

Henry Reynolds thinks that these Aboriginal women may have gone to European men willingly – or actually sought them out – either to escape undesired marriage or tribal punishment, or to gain access to the many attractive possessions the Europeans had. It is important to remember, however, that these relationships took place against a background of continual frontier and sexual violence. This was an environment in which resources were scarce, times were tough and options were few.

Ann McGrath explains how Aboriginal women (and Aboriginal men) were quick to understand the importance of economic power in this era of change. Aboriginal women did assert power and agency within the colonial context, and they could participate in the new marketplace. According to anthropologist Diane Barwick, Aboriginal women had a range of choices available to them in colonial society. As she writes in a chapter of *Women's Role in Aboriginal Society*, 'And the Lubras Are Ladies Now':

They were admitted more readily into the central living quarters of these stations, to undertake various domestic tasks, including the care of young children.

They were regarded generally as more biddable, more submissive, easier to keep under control. Their opportunities for observation of new things and new ways were more numerous; and so, up to a point, were their opportunities for acquisition and imitation.

In pre-invasion society, Aboriginal women had a level of political power. Under colonial rule, this radically changed, and they had no political power in post-invasion society. There is a silence within colonial narratives about the contribution of Indigenous women to the development of the modern Australian state. Intertwined with the exploitation of Aboriginal women's sexuality on the frontier was the exploitation of Aboriginal women's labour. The colonists needed it and, like the use and abuse of Aboriginal women's sexuality, it attracted a silence that allowed their role to be forgotten in the folklore of the fledgling nation.

While white women on the frontier were romanticised in iconic tales such as Mrs Aeneas Gunn's *We of the Never-Never*, the presence and the work of Aboriginal women were eclipsed by the emphasis on and elevation of the contribution of their white counterparts. In the written histories, there is seldom recognition of the contribution of Aboriginal women. Yet Indigenous women had substantial parts to play in the pearling industry, the pastoral industry and in domestic service. As midwives in remote areas, they assisted European women and babies. They worked hard, were highly skilled and thus indispensable. Despite the often arduous tasks and long hours, they were unpaid or underpaid. As Henry Reynolds notes in *Why Weren't We Told?*:

> *A Queensland government official who visited a large number of stations in the south-west of the colony in 1900 found only two cases where the women were paid anything at all, even though the station owners admitted that their black servants did work for which they would have paid a white woman fifteen shillings or one pound a week.*

The extent to which Aboriginal women consented to labour and sexual relations needs to be considered against the backdrop of power relations within colonial society. Aboriginal women may have used the 'gin spree' as a source of income. They may also have understood the advantages of a sexual liaison with 'the boss' as it provided a form of protection and economic security for themselves and their family.

Violence towards Aboriginal people was close to the surface in frontier and colonial society. If Aboriginal women had not bargained an assent, it is open to question whether any notice would have been taken of their refusals since in so many instances it was not. Indeed, free and open consent within the colonial context is questionable if you consider the physical power and duress used by colonisers to clear land and control Indigenous people they needed or wanted for labour and sexual gratification.

Despite its prevalence, sexual contact with Aboriginal

women was treated as socially abhorrent by white society. Aboriginal women were considered highly sexualised but socially untouchable, and became mistresses or prostitutes more often than legal wives; their children often went unacknowledged. The legitimisation of a relationship between a white man and a black woman through marriage came to be seen as especially dangerous to the developing colony. In the Northern Territory in the 1910s and 1920s, it became necessary for a white man to obtain the permission of the Protector in order to marry an Aboriginal woman. Permission to marry was rarely granted. This legislation penalised men who were in long-term, more open relationships with Aboriginal women, yet it did nothing to prevent white men from using Aboriginal women as casual sexual partners. And it was thought unimaginable that a white woman would want to marry an Aboriginal man.

However, the laws against cohabitation were extremely difficult to enforce and the police frequently sympathised with the offenders, especially as many police officers were single men who had Aboriginal girlfriends themselves. Even so, liaisons between black women and white men, regardless of their nature, do not appear in either nationalistic imagery or frontier mythology. While white women could achieve elevated social status and economic mobility through marriage, this path to respectability and gentility was impossible for Aboriginal women, which only perpetuated the myth that white women were superior to and more desirable than their Aboriginal counterparts.

The folktales of iconic Australian RM Williams

show that the proprietary, sexualising attitude towards Aboriginal women in the outback was not just a construct of first contact but reflected notions that became firmly entrenched throughout the twentieth century. Williams's autobiographical tales highlight the assumed ownership of Aboriginal labour:

> *I knew Ruth later – her real name was Molly Lennon and her benefactors gave her to my wife as a servant. We kept her until she married a boy …*

Williams also candidly alludes to his lust:

> *The stockmen that I fraternised with along the way were envious of the chance to meet the nude ladies of the wild tribes – they would risk a spear, they said. Wade couldn't stop me looking but he put strict limits on his conscience …*

The popular portrayal of inter-race relationships was one of tongue-in-cheek slyness. An example of this assumption of access veiled with the pretext of request for consent is portrayed in the following poem, originally published in *The Bulletin* in 1882:

> *O blackfellows, you look like men,*
> *And should be, therefore, of our kin:*
> *We give you rum and faith. What then?*
> *You'll surely spare us a small gin.*

The constructions of 'Empire' and 'savage', of 'Christian' and 'heathen', of 'civilised' and 'barbaric' that appear in stories like Eliza Fraser's created distinctions between European and Aboriginal Australians. They reinforced an 'us' and 'them' dichotomy and, by making this distinction, treated Aboriginal people as different – as 'other' – but also asserted that they were culturally and biologically inferior.

The value judgements and ideologies embedded in the Eliza Fraser story mirrored those that were prevalent in colonial society, including in the legal system. By creating two different classes of people, colonial laws sanctioned different treatment too.

The 'savagery' of Aboriginal people as it was represented in stories such as Eliza Fraser's helped to propagate the idea that Aboriginal people needed to be tamed. When this wasn't achieved through 'retaliatory' lethal violence or atrocities against Aboriginal women, it was done through the implementation of the policies of assimilation and dispossession or by controlling Aboriginal people within their segregated communities on reserves and missions.

These stereotypes legitimised the existence of the government's regulations and policies. In turn, the law worked to legitimise and entrench those beliefs, whether by ignoring genocidal acts, the theft of Aboriginal land or the regulation of Aboriginal life through the Aborigines Protection Board.

If the 'savagery' of Aboriginal people was justification

for surveillance, control and regulation, the 'savagery' of Aboriginal cultural practices enabled colonists to overlook the relationship that Aboriginal people had with their land. Eliza's narrative says nothing of the Butchulla's spiritual attachment to their land. Instead, the Butchulla are portrayed as a nomadic primitive society – and this misconception fed the legal fiction of *terra nullius*.

The government policies of segregation and assimilation were both pursued by state governments. In New South Wales, responsibility for these policies fell to the Aborigines Protection Board, established in 1883. The Board regulated the lives of Aboriginal people, exercising control over association, movement, employment and food. This control worked hand in hand with the removal of children. By controlling the conditions on missions and reserves, the government was responsible for the squalor and malnutrition that plagued many Aboriginal communities. Those living conditions then became the grounds upon which to remove children from their families. In their book, *The Lost Children*, Coral Edwards and Peter Read write that even those who 'blamed the government for the squalor that Aboriginal people lived in thought it still might be best that the child, for its own sake, should grow up in a comfortable suburban home'.

Read also notes in his book *A Rape of the Soul So Profound: The Return of the Stolen Generations* that the negative attitudes towards Aboriginality were so deeply entrenched that to non-Aboriginal people 'separation seemed preferable to almost any divergence from the

European nuclear family model'. The provision for the removal of children remained on the books until 1969 in New South Wales. Through this policy, Aboriginal children were forcibly removed; they were in effect kidnapped, captured.

ANOTHER GENUINE FRONTIER CAPTIVITY STORY

This surveillance and control created yet another genuine colonial captivity narrative. I have reconstructed the following from testimonies contained within the Human Rights and Equal Opportunity Commission's report *Bringing Them Home*. These accounts are harrowing and, even after so many years, the pain and trauma are evident. It is striking how the evidence from people who had been taken as children, when put together, creates a tale that includes the very same dangers and perils that Eliza Fraser claimed she suffered. In most cases, however, they were real and much worse.

... captured by savages ...

They put us in the police ute and said they were taking us to Broome. They put the mums in there as well. But when we'd gone about ten miles they stopped, and threw the mothers out of the car. We jumped on our mothers' backs, crying, trying not to be left behind. But the policemen pulled us off and threw us in the back of the car. They pushed the mothers away and drove off, while our mothers were chasing the car, running and crying after us. We were screaming in the back of that car.

... suffered cruel abuse at the hands of the savages ...

There was no food, nothing. We was all huddled up in a room like a little puppy dog on the floor. Sometimes at night we'd cry with hunger. We had to scrounge in the town dump, eating old bread, smashing tomato sauce bottles, licking them. Half of the time the food we got was from the rubbish dump.

Dormitory life was like living in hell. It was not a life. The only things that sort of come out of it was how to work, how to be clean, you know and hygiene. That sort of thing. But we got a lot of bashings.

... treated like slaves ...

We never got our wages. It was banked for us. And when we were 21 we were supposed to get this money. We never got any of that money ever. And that's what I wonder: where could that money have went? Or why didn't we get it?

... suffered a fate worse than death ...

There was tampering with the boys ... the people who would come in to work with the children, they would grab the boys' penises, play around with them and kiss them and things like this. These were the things that were done ... It was seen to be the white man's way of looking after you. It never happened with an Aboriginal.

I ran away because my foster father used to tamper with me and I'd just had enough. I went to the police but they didn't believe me. So she [foster mother] just thought I was a wild child and she put me into one of those hostels and none of them believed me – I was the liar. So I've never talked about it to anyone. I don't go about telling lies, especially big lies like that.

5

Fictionalising Aboriginal Women

WHILE ELIZA FRASER'S story is one in which Aboriginal women are demonised, it is just as interesting to look at the way in which negative stereotypes creep into books that were intended to show some empathy for Aboriginal people.

Capture and sexual danger comprise the dominant narrative for Indigenous women who suffered through the process of colonisation and have been left a lasting legacy in their low socio-economic status. This treatment has been reinforced and naturalised by colonial narratives – both literary and legal. Even the 'sympathetic' accounts of Aboriginal people reveal much more about colonial roles, ideas and relation to land than they do about Indigenous women and their families. These stories reiterate stereotypes and societal perceptions and are far from harmless tales. They continue to have an enormous impact on the lives and bodies of Indigenous women in contemporary Australia.

A MISCEGENATION MORALITY TALE:
KATHARINE SUSANNAH PRICHARD'S *COONARDOO*

When I was in high school in suburban Sydney in the 1980s, one of the names I was called was 'Coonardoo', with the emphasis being placed on the first four letters. This was the title of a novel taught to some of the English classes (not mine). I never worried too much about the label because, as a black woman, there are worse names that you can be called. It was only when I went to study at Harvard and took to borrowing Australian novels from the undergraduate library to lessen my homesickness that I finally picked up a copy of this namesake book. I was horrified when I realised the implications of being called 'Coonardoo', of the images and messages that had been placed upon me with this name.

Coonardoo was said to be a novel ahead of its time for its portrayal of the relationship between Coonardoo, an Aboriginal woman, and Hugh 'Hughie' Watt, son and heir of a pastoral lessee. First published in 1928 in *The Bulletin*, Prichard's book scandalised readers with its portrayal of a so-called 'love relationship' between a white and an Aborigine.

Coonardoo and her tribe live on Wytaliba, their traditional land and now a station 'owned' by the Watts. Hugh and Coonardoo are childhood playmates. As they grow, Hugh goes away to school, and Coonardoo works in the homestead on the station and out on the property with the men. She is also married to Warieda, a much older Aboriginal man.

After his schooling, Hugh returns to Wytaliba, groomed for his role in taking over from his mother. When Mrs Bessie, Hugh's mother, passes away, a grief-stricken Hugh turns to Coonardoo for solace. After this sexual encounter, Hugh becomes sick and leaves the station. In his absence, Coonardoo gives birth to Winni, her son to Hugh. When Hugh returns to the station, with him is Mollie, his white wife.

Coonardoo continues to work as housekeeper at Wytaliba, through the birth of Hugh and Mollie's children, the eventual breakdown of Hugh's marriage, and Mollie's departure to Geraldton. When Coonardoo's husband dies, Hugh decides to take Coonardoo as his 'wife' to prevent Sam Geary, an adjacent landowner who openly lives with his 'gins', from taking her. Even though Coonardoo is now 'his woman', Hugh does not resume a sexual relationship with her.

One night, when Hugh is away from the house, Sam Geary arrives and 'seduces' Coonardoo. When Hugh discovers the encounter, Coonardoo is banished from Wytaliba. When she finally returns to die, Wytaliba is deserted. Hugh has lost the property to the banks and her own people have moved elsewhere.

THE IRON HAND IN THE VELVET GLOVE

Mrs Bessie's philosophy towards her Aborigines is clearly stated:

Mother handled them extraordinarily well. It's the iron hand in the velvet glove that does the trick, she used to say. Was very strict about some things. Respected them and their ideas. Made 'em respect her. If they wanted the things she had to give, she made them do what she wanted, obey her, wash, and not take anything without asking. They're naturally honest ... fair dealers.

Her benevolent attitude towards her Aborigines is tempered when she finds aspects of Aboriginal culture unpalatable. At these moments she cannot help but intervene, 'saving' Coonardoo from marriage at a young age and taking the young girl to work in the homestead kitchen.

With hindsight, Mrs Bessie's role may be seen as a parody of the benevolent caregiver, the misguided liberal. However, Prichard approved of the condescending benevolence of Mrs Bessie. Through Coonardoo, Prichard asserts that white landowners like the Watts have a duty to care for their Aborigines and treat them well, and if they abandon that duty, it leads to their own destruction and dispossession. This is evident in the miserable fate Coonardoo suffers when she leaves the 'protective' environment of the white-owned station – and in Prichard's attack of Sam Geary's rather than the Watts' treatment of Aboriginal women.

The exploitation of Aboriginal labour under the guise of Hugh and Bessie's supposed benevolence is tangible.

Mrs Bessie teaches Coonardoo the management of the household and threatens her with haunting and fearful 'guts-ache' if she lets Hugh down, no matter what happens.

In order to research her novel, Prichard spent over two months in 1926 on Turee Creek Station in north-west Western Australia. Nevertheless, the book ignores the greater aspects of violence and duress that kept Aboriginal people in a state of dependence on pastoralists from the time their lands were colonised to well into the twentieth century. At the time Prichard wrote *Coonardoo*, the 'killing times' were fresh in the minds of Aboriginal people.

In 1928, the year *Coonardoo* was serialised in *The Bulletin*, Mounted Constable William George Murray swept through the area around Coniston in the Northern Territory, killing on sight. The massacre had been in 'retaliation' for the death of a white dingo trapper, Fred Brooks. According to the local Aborigines, Brooks was speared because he had failed to meet obligations in return for Aboriginal women. The Warlpiri estimate that between sixty and seventy people were killed, though the official count was only seventeen. Murray himself confessed that he thought the number closer to seventy. He claimed that all those shot had been killed in self-defence and had been implicated in the murder of a white man. Later that year, Murray led another killing spree that saw a further hundred Aboriginal people killed, but once again the official count was far lower – only fourteen.

This violence is far from the minds of the Aboriginal people in Prichard's idyllic Wytaliba when in fact, for

Aborigines at that time in Western Australia and the Northern Territory, 'punitive expeditions' were a fearful reality. Many Aboriginal people came to missions or developed relationships where they could work on pastoral properties in order to be protected from violence on the frontier. This recent history of violent frontier encounters, along with the backdrop it provides to black–white relations, is missing from the pages of Prichard's novel.

TREAT THEM GENEROUSLY, FEED THEM WELL

In Prichard's novel, Hugh inherits both his mother's land and her benevolent attitude towards the Aboriginal people on the station:

> *But these people are not servants … We don't pay them, except in food, tobacco, clothing. Treat them generously, feed them well – Give them a bit of pain killer or a dose of castor oil when they've got a bingee ache, and they'll do anything in the world for you – especially the gins.*

Coonardoo becomes ostensibly a slave in the Wytaliba kitchen but she also does the men's work. She is the provider for her own family in a camp that is rarely referred to in the book, as though her whole life could revolve only around the homestead kitchen rather than her family and the land that she loves. And then, all this work is diminished by the perpetuation of the myth that Aboriginal women are lazy.

They're not made for hard work, can't stand it. Look at their little hands – Coonardoo's – I've never seen any woman with as little hands as Coonardoo.

In this novel, it is not the use of slave labour itself that is drawn into question, but the abuse of the inherent superiority that is criticised. Prichard again highlights the duty of white landowners to care for their Aborigines and it is those who abuse that assumed authority, men like Sam Geary, who are the recipients of her ire. Prichard highlights the difference in the use of the power – benevolence as opposed to abuse – of the landowner but never questions the assertion of that authority.

MARRYING WHITE AND STICKING WHITE

Despite a supposed 'love-relationship', Hugh shows little interest in Coonardoo's feelings and her circumstances. Any feelings he has for her are suppressed within his racial bigotry: 'I'm goin' to marry white and stick white.' He maintains this especially in the face of Sam Geary's taunts: 'No stud gins for me – no matter what happens.' Before she dies, Mrs Bessie reinforces her disapproval: 'It'll be lonely when I'm gone. I don't want you mucking around with the gins.' So Hugh swears himself off Coonardoo: '… sentimental about a gin, Hugh had promised himself never to be.'

However, heartbroken by his mother's death, Hugh turns to Coonardoo for consolation. His 'playmate' is a source of compassion and tenderness but, in the light of day, Hugh rejects her and is ashamed of sleeping with her. He becomes ill and leaves, returning with a white wife, leaving Coonardoo to give birth to his child in his absence.

Mollie, Hugh's wife, is a working-class woman and quick to take her role in Wytaliba as mistress. She asserts her proprietorship over the home and its assets, including Coonardoo:

> *She would show Hugh how a house should be run, and the gins too ... This slow, lazy, go-as-you-please way of doing things would not suit her ... For the first time in her life Mollie had a sense of ownership. Her proprietorship in this kitchen, these pots and pans ...*

Hugh and Mollie use their economic power and skin-colour privilege to control and exploit the Aboriginal people whose land they are living upon. Prichard does draw out the complicity of white women like Mollie in the exploitation of Aboriginal women as Coonardoo plays maid and nursemaid to Hugh, his wife and their children.

A STICK, OR A BOOT, HE WOULD ONLY USE ON A GIN

The novel also acknowledges that white women were treated differently from Aboriginal women.

> *... Coonardoo heard Joey Koonarra suggesting Hugh should take a stick to Mollie. But that was not the*

white man's way, she knew. He might take her by the shoulders and shake her til her neck was nearly broken, or put his hands around her throat, threatening to strangle her. But a stick, or a boot, he would only use on a gin. Mollie would never get those.

During this time Winni, only later to be a source of some pride, is not acknowledged by Hugh, though Mollie, growing increasingly disgruntled with station life over the years, figures out the connection:

And she saw Hugh stamped all over him … His features were aboriginal certainly, but with a refinement.

This knowledge becomes a powerful weapon for the frustrated Mollie:

Mollie knew her Nor'-West well enough to know that on this subject most men lied to their wives … She realised her knowledge would mean power.

Even though the union with Coonardoo occurred before Hugh had met Mollie, his contact with Coonardoo is an eternal stain in the eyes of white society.

Of course, Mollie was entitled to feel herself outraged. The women in Geraldton would agree with her when she told them the story.

Mollie uses the liaison with Coonardoo as an excuse to leave Wytaliba for life in Geraldton.

When Coonardoo's husband, Warieda, dies, Hugh steps in, just as his mother had, to interfere with tribal law that would make Warieda's brother responsible for looking after her. Instead, Hugh claims Coonardoo as 'his wife' – which means allowing her to sleep on his verandah. But Hugh does not take her as a lover, and Coonardoo is confused and hurt by his physical rejection of her.

Phyllis, Hugh's daughter, returns to the homestead and is wooed by a white pastoralist, Bill Gale. These characters provide a social commentary on Hugh's behaviour towards Coonardoo and towards Aboriginal women in general:

> *I'm not shook on gins myself. They're a repulsive lot, mostly. Not that I've been any better than most men who've lived a long time in this country, Phyll.*

Phyllis observes that Winni is her stepbrother and that 'Coonardoo and Winni, as far as Hugh's concerned, were an accident'. Bill's reply is that 'Gins are, as a rule.' Unlike Geary, who openly lives with his 'gins', Bill, although admitting to past weakness, would never consider one as a partner: 'A man doesn't love a gin, not a white man.' It is Phyllis who observes that Hugh's repression of his feelings for Coonardoo 'have rotted him out'.

On a night when Hugh is away, his nemesis, Sam Geary, who has long desired Coonardoo, arrives and 'seduces' her after offering her alcohol. Coonardoo is wary of Geary, whom she has always despised.

> *Disturbed and apprehensive, she moved out of the range of Geary's eyes. She saw in them what she had always seen.*

Despite her lifetime of disgust for Geary, Coonardoo is weakened, 'half dead in her sterility'. Geary and his friend argue over who will have Coonardoo:

> *'No.' Geary's voice, thick and insistent, soared and foundered. 'Coonardoo's mine. You can have Bardi.' …*
>
> *They had got Bardi. Coonardoo heard her struggling, crying out, giggling and exclaiming.*

(Bardi's 'no' apparently means 'yes'.)

> *Heavy and drunken, in the doorway, his eyes glazed, Geary stood swaying, an old man with his hair on end, his face red, swollen and ugly. Coonardoo could have moved past and away from him in the darkness. But she did not move. As weak and fascinated as a bird before a snake she swayed*

there for Geary whom she had loathed and feared
beyond any human being. Yet male to her female,
she could not resist him. Her need of him was as
great as the dry earth for rain.

So Coonardoo, weak and fascinated, is seduced by Geary, whose drunken assertion and assumption of proprietorship are established before Coonardoo has even consented. When Hugh discovers that Geary 'took Coonardoo' that night, he becomes violent towards her, cruelly burning her in the campfire when she tries to cling to him. He then banishes her from Wytaliba, the place of her birth, family and home. No questions are asked about Coonardoo's consent to the encounter despite her lifelong animosity towards Geary and his many sly attempts, including an attempted abduction, to secure her for himself. Hugh is criticised not for his assumption of consent, but for his overreaction to Coonardoo's apparent transgression.

While it was understood a black should treat a gin
who behaved badly like that, they could not
understand Hugh doing the same sort of thing.

Winni drags his mother from the fire but Coonardoo is badly burnt. She disappears and the remaining members of her clan begin to act as though she is dead. The house becomes neglected as Hugh waits for her to come back, feeling grief and remorse:

Coonardoo, my poor Coonardoo, if you'd been a dog
I wouldn't have treated you like that ...

Coonardoo wanders to the coast, diseased with leprosy. In her absence, the station becomes unprofitable and no longer viable. Wytaliba is taken by the banks, and it will eventually end up in the hands of Sam Geary. Hugh goes fossicking with Cock-Eyed Bob. Coonardoo comes back to die on Wytaliba. Her people are gone, the homestead deserted and the land no longer sustaining life.

Coonardoo is named after 'the well in the shadows'. She is an embodiment of the life spirit, a symbol for the life source for her land and for her people. When Hugh drives Coonardoo away from Wytaliba, the well dries up. Her death represents the fate of her people and the inevitable destruction of her country.

She also symbolises Hugh's failure to fulfil his obligations to protect and care for her and her people. Her life is a morality tale of what happens when Aborigines are neglected by a benevolent landowner. Historian John Docker sums this up when he observes that in *Coonardoo*:

White civilisation is perceived as thin and artificial because it has lost touch with the vitality of the natural world, a vitality enjoyed by and symbolised in the noble Australian 'primitive'.

If Coonardoo is a symbol of primitive natural vitality, Hugh is a symbol of European civilisation. Prichard warns that Hugh needs to embrace this vitality in order to come to terms with his place on Australian soil. To me, *Coonardoo* feels like an attempt to reconcile the white relationship to the land and the Aboriginal people who are displaced from it. It does not seek to liberate or empower Aboriginal people.

There are many who defend Prichard's novel. Jack Beasley, who wrote *The Rage for Life: The Work of Katharine Susannah Prichard*, calls it 'the first adequate characterisation of an Aborigine in our literature'. However, as I see it, the most disappointing aspect of the book is that although it has Aboriginal characters, they are in fact merely symbolic. If we feel sympathy for Coonardoo, it is because we mourn the fate of the people she symbolises or Hugh's treatment of her, not because we feel any connection to her. It is the white people who are the story, and in their actions lies the moral of the tale. As leading literary scholar Harry Heseltine observes in *Acquainted with the Night: Studies in Classic Australian Fiction*:

> ... *too much of Coonardoo's personal psychology is given to us in ... statements about, rather than dramatisations of, her situation and personality. As a result, she becomes rather more a paradigm of an elected type than a fully realised fictional character, a paradigm elected to suit the author's programmatic purpose of writing a serious and tragic novel with an aboriginal protagonist.*

Despite claims that the book was ahead of its time because of its portrayal of a relationship between an Aboriginal woman and a white man, *Coonardoo* is trapped within a self-reflective moment when European Australians began to realise the enormity of the destruction they had wrought upon Aboriginal communities, livelihoods and lives. This is a story about white sorrow, not black empowerment. Prichard's book omits any possibility that Coonardoo and her community could benefit from the assertion of their own authority or autonomy.

> *This is a story about white sorrow, not black empowerment.*

Some critics would argue that this analysis is too harsh on Prichard and that critics like me forget that it is the love between Hugh and Coonardoo that is the author's focus. Prichard claimed many years later that her intention with the novel was to draw attention to the mistreatment of Aboriginal women by white men like Sam Geary.

Indeed, Sam Geary makes no secret of his desire for Coonardoo – and for Wytaliba. He is totally unaffected by the 'moral code' of the whites which has wrought such deep division in the character of Hugh. He triumphs in the end. The treatment of 'his' 'gins' is a source of irritation to Mollie. She believes that the way Geary treats them is far too good for them, and that it is she who should be getting the fine clothing and jewellery; in short, Mollie is jealous of their trappings as kept women.

To complicate matters, for over two or three years, Geary has had a common-law wife, an Aboriginal woman named Sheba, who is included in his social circle. Sheba travels with him and attends to the duties in the house. However, at Wytaliba, there is no recognition of their relationship. Sheba is sent to eat with 'the other gins' and stays by the ration cart while Geary visits the Watts, waiting in the shadows until it is time to go. What the Watts reject is the elevation of Aboriginal women through colonial structures, the very structures that are exploiting them and placing them in subordinated positions. Prichard states that the 'Wytaliba women laughed at, exclaimed over, but did not envy Sheba'. They reject the trappings and advantages of sexual exploitation though apparently they embrace the drudgery that comes with the exploitation of their labour. At Wytaliba, the exploitation of Aboriginal women comes without cost to the property owners, who get all the same advantages from using them just as Sam Geary does.

If Prichard's attitude to Sam Geary is critical, her attitude to Hugh is more ambivalent. Anyone who understood the violence and duress levelled against Aboriginal women on the frontier would be suspicious of the 'love-relationship' between Hugh and Coonardoo, especially since she is not given any agency or personality within the book. Instead, her character is defined by her submissiveness. It is assumed that Coonardoo will want Hugh – and it is assumed that the Aborigines on the property will be loyal to the 'new' owners. The repercussions for saying 'no' are absent from the book, providing no context for the environment in which Aboriginal women and their families had to live and make their choices.

A throwaway line in the book mentions the circumstances in which Coonardoo's mother, Maria, died after Hugh's father 'kicked her off the verandah' during a drunken spree for answering back and refusing to carry out an order. This is the underlying message to Aboriginal women about the violence they will encounter if they are not submissive and obedient. In the text, there is no further reference to this incident, which would have provided a profound psychological lesson to Coonardoo about saying 'yes' or 'no' to the Watts.

Add to this the frontier violence beyond the boundaries of the benevolent property owner, and the context in which sexual consent is sought offers little actual free choice. In Coonardoo's case, there is the additional threat of the 'guts-ache' if she should ever 'let Hugh down'. Coonardoo's 'consent' occurs within the very real and violent colonial constraints, but Prichard seems to lack an understanding of the limits placed upon the agency of a woman in Coonardoo's position.

Hugh Watt's power as landowner – his legal right – allows him to banish Coonardoo from his property, and this shows the enormity of the power that he has always had over her. The fact that he thinks she will come back is evidence that he does not understand the authority he has over Aboriginal people nor the callous thoughtlessness with which this can be used.

Jack Beasley sees the novel as highlighting the fact that the 'destruction of Coonardoo and the Gnarler people was accomplished not by the vicious exterminators of the Aborigines, but by the kindly, well-meaning exploiters, the Watt family'. He reads *Coonardoo* as one of the first books to recognise that it is not only the Sam Gearys of the country who are to be condemned, but the 'Hugh Watts, those who exploit in the name of respect, those who love, but will not own to that love'.

Prichard's criticism targets the paternalistic abuse of power. She does not, however, advocate the emancipation and decolonisation of Aboriginal people and notions of land rights and citizenship – blossoming political rights movements within Indigenous communities when the book was penned. There is not even a hint of such things in her text. Instead, *Coonardoo* adopts a righteous tone of self-reflection at the inability of white Australians to come to terms with the land and the people they have a moral and spiritual duty to protect.

Though some may read *Coonardoo* as a reminder of the loves lost because of racism, the novel is also a reminder of the unacknowledged legacy of colonisation on Aboriginal women: their ability to freely consent to sexual relations with the white men who had the power of life and death over them was fundamentally constrained. It is also a reminder that, regardless of any good intention, constructed stereotypes of Aboriginal men and women continue to appear and be perpetuated in even so-called 'sympathetic' twenty-first-century literature.

A CONTEMPORARY RE-IMAGINING OF THE CAPTURED WHITE WOMAN

Australian author Liam Davison produced a post-colonial interpretation of the frontier captivity narrative in his powerful 1994 novel, *The White Woman*. Drawing inspiration from another myth of a white woman 'captured' by 'savages', Davison's novel provides a deep understanding of what propelled these types of narratives.

In the 1840s, rumours circulated of sightings of a white woman living with Aboriginal people in the Gippsland region of Victoria. These whisperings increased in 1841 when a party of white men disturbed an encampment of Aboriginal people near Port Albert and found an article of European female clothing. At least two major expeditions set out to find and rescue the unknown, unnamed woman to whom the item belonged. The search parties found nothing, but a contemporary estimation puts the number of Aborigines killed in the course of the search at fifty.

Davison's novel tells this story from the perspective of a member of the search parties, who years later reflects on his motivations and the ideologies that urged him to join the expedition. Through this fictional reconstruction, Davison explores themes of the colonial agenda, the amorphous nature of 'truth' and the victor's version of history. He also explores the white woman as a symbol of the Empire and delves into the paternalistic attitudes that white male frontiersmen held about white women. He highlights the fantasy of playing the 'saviour' with all of its sexual undertones. He is sensitive to the way in which this construct of white femininity places the Aboriginal woman in the position of the feminine and sexual 'other'.

> *She was perfect, as I'd always imagined her to be ... I believed I could have saved her from it all if she'd only come to me ... She was mine you see, long before the expedition set out ...*
>
> *My faith in her was complete ...*
>
> *She wanted us. She longed for us to take her. I put my arms around her, pulled her gently towards me to shield her from any further degradation she might expect from the hands of men ... the way her body trembled against me, her quick breaths ... So vulnerable. So utterly dependent on us.*

Davison explores the sexual exploitation of Aboriginal women through graphic symbolism – rather than graphic violence – in a scene where the search party thinks it spies the 'white woman'. Through this scene, he illustrates how the black woman is constructed by society to be made into a 'poorer' version of the white woman; that the model of femininity that she is made to aspire to – and is trapped by – is the one defined by white women.

And as she kept moving closer, almost stumbling into us, I saw that she wasn't white at all but black. She was hideously daubed with thick white paint that matted her eyebrows and hair and flaked like scabs from her cheeks so her own dark skin showed through like bruises against the white. Her eyes were tormented by it, reddened around their edges and barely able to close. And her hands! Her wrists showed black where the sleeves of the dress rode up. Her knuckles were caked with it. How long she'd endured it, I couldn't say. What other tasks she had been coerced into performing to realise his pitiful delusions, we could only guess. There was a knitted bag tied to her wrist, the filthy remains of a bonnet looped around her neck. The book she held was grubby beyond belief, as if she'd been forced to carry it with her always.

As his expedition travels deeper inland, Davison's narrator discovers the dark deeds committed on the frontier. The horror becomes more apparent and, increasingly, the need to keep it covered up, to tell a different version of history, becomes all the more imperative. What is unveiled as the expedition continues on its mission is the true barbarity underpinning colonisation and the savage history behind places with names like 'Boney Point' and 'Butchers Ridge'.

History you'll call it, all the more truthful for having all the angles; all the more sceptical ... No doubt you'll alter it to suit, or choose what you want to hear – which bits will become history and which will not. I'll tell you my truth anyway for what it's worth; the truth I hold to ...

It wasn't so much lies that shaped our accounts of what went on out there as silence ...

Better not scratch too deep I think ...

I wasn't with your father then, but I saw the signs of where he'd been – broken carbine clotted with hair and skin, the trampled grass, the bodies lying in the bush ...

Wouldn't it be easier to talk of the butchery of your own people? Because they weren't white all, those bones ... Every one was black. All shot or beaten with heavy sticks.

'It wasn't so much lies that shaped our accounts of what went on out there as silence ...'

As the men in the expedition party come to understand the scale of frontier slaughter and the depth of its barbarity, their need to find the white woman becomes all the more urgent. There has to be a justification for the brutality they've encountered, and 'the captured white woman' can provide it.

As the search becomes more desperate, the creeping fear that the 'white woman' does not exist becomes stronger. The search party hears that a white woman has been sighted on a beach. They rush to find her, only to discover a ship's figurehead: the torso of the white woman Britannia, symbol of Empire, imperialism and colonial expansion.

It was lying half-concealed near what was once a native camp with some broken spears and the burnt remains of a flannel shirt. The gun was broken off at the stock and there was a clump of black hair, all clotted with blood, about the lock. Do you know what force it takes to break a gun like that? It isn't done lightly.

Still, we danced with joy to find it. Yes, danced. What exhilaration as we lifted it shoulder high and felt its rough wood against our backs. Yes, we brought it in – would have carried it to Melbourne if we could. How self-satisfied we felt, how proud. How it made up for all we'd been through – to be bearing Britannia back to civilization.

Davison provides a graphic metaphor for the constructed opposites between black and white women:

> *Dolls. Identical paper dolls flapping from his hands like handkerchiefs as he walked towards the fire ... Then he rubbed the charcoal over one of them, carefully at first, gentle even, caressing the white paper as if he didn't want to tear it. He started at the head and worked down – shoulders, breasts, waist. And the more discoloured the doll became, the harder he rubbed, smeared the black stuff over it with all his spit and grinding the hard point of his stick against it ... In his other hand was the white doll – untouched, pristine – and he held that out too ... he folded it (the white doll) carefully into his pocket like it was a ten pound note. The other he tossed onto the fire.*

Katharine Susannah Prichard was a fiercely intellectual woman who thought deeply about the society of her time. She understood that Australians had to deal with the problems of Aboriginal people and she attempted to make her strongest statement about this issue through her fiction.

It is easy to dismiss the patronising aspects of *Coonardoo* as a reflection of Prichard's time, but the novel is also evidence of something more. Successful storytelling requires the writer to create characters that ring true – whether in historical fiction, romance or science fiction. As readers, we have to believe in their authenticity. And you cannot create an authentic Aboriginal character unless you are able to deeply and truly understand their experience and perspective. In the 1920s, when Prichard was writing, the last people to be asked about how issues facing Indigenous people should be dealt with were Aboriginal and Torres Strait Islander people themselves. They simply weren't included in public discourse. Prichard could research her novel by visiting pastoral properties in Western Australia, but it is not surprising that the story is strongest when it critiques the behaviour of pastoralists and weakest when it seeks to create multi-dimensional Aboriginal characters.

In *The White Woman*, on the other hand, Davison writes knowing that he can articulate the psyche of the colonist and tell a story about motivation and mindset from that point of view. The fact that he does not feel compelled to tell any or all events from an Indigenous perspective does not in any way weaken his story; it only makes it stronger. Davison understands one of the key messages in the Eliza Fraser captivity narrative – that while such stories teach us nothing about the Aboriginal point of view, they can teach us much about the colonial one. And yet, the overall feel of his novel is one that is imbued with a natural sympathy and compassion for what Aboriginal people faced in the Gippsland region.

6

Cannibalism:
Dark Acts on the Frontier

AFTER THE *STIRLING CASTLE* was wrecked, Captain Fraser was reluctant to land his longboat because he was certain Australia was inhabited by cannibals and he feared they would eat him. He preferred to stay afloat and only agreed to come ashore after his crew threatened to 'draw lots' and eat someone.

As Captain Fraser's hypocrisy shows, Europeans viewed the uncolonised parts of the world with a prejudice that was deeply rooted in their own dark acts. He was not alone. Most of Eliza Fraser's chroniclers assumed that cannibalism was a common cultural practice of the Aboriginal people. Consider Michael Alexander's description in *Mrs Fraser and the Fatal Shore*:

> *The grotesque elder, who was some sort of witch doctor, approached with an air of immense self-importance, laid hold of Captain Fraser's chin, and rubbed his hands up and down his naked body as if*

establishing tangibility, and then his qualities as a work-horse or even, Captain Fraser would probably have felt, a future meal.

John Curtis in his *Shipwreck of the Stirling Castle* describes an Aboriginal 'corroboree' in the following salacious terms:

> *… they might escape unobserved during a midnight revel of the natives, called a 'Corrobery', which is a merry-making, and consists of dancing in a circle round a favourite friend, but more frequently perhaps round a miserable captive, whose flesh they would presently greedily devour.*

Eliza Fraser was not just in danger of suffering the 'fate worse than death'; she was in danger of becoming dinner. As Eliza's most devoted chronicler, Curtis avoids mentioning the rumours that circulated in Sydney that lost members of the *Stirling Castle* crew had been eaten by their shipmates. However, he does refer to instances of cannibalism among survivors of other shipwrecks and shows that there was a certain tolerance of the consumption of human flesh in that context.

The Butchulla were not cannibals. Darge, a member of the *Stirling Castle* crew, contradicted the accounts of cannibalism by other survivors at a London inquiry. He said he had seen no evidence of the practice among the Aboriginal people he had been in contact with. But the morbid fascination with and fear of cannibalism seemed hard to shake in Europeans. Even accounts sympathetic to Aboriginal people were quick to try to place the practice in a context rather than to question whether it ever existed at all.

In Patrick White's *A Fringe of Leaves*, an act of cannibalism is used to symbolise spiritual communion as Ellen (the character based on Eliza Fraser) reconnects with and embraces her sensual, primitive self. When Ellen, uninvited, comes across the performance of funeral rites for an Aboriginal child, she can see from the 'greasy smears on lips and cheeks how the flesh had disappeared' from the body of the child. In response to this discovery, Ellen feels a range of emotions including fear, amazement, disgust and pity. She looks down and catches sight of a thigh bone, and although her initial reaction is to kick the bone out of sight, uncontrollably, she partakes of the practice:

> *Then, instead, she found herself stooping, to pick it up. There were one or two shreds of half-cooked flesh and gobbets of burnt fat still adhering to this monstrous object. Her stiffened body and almost audibly twangling nerves were warning her against what she was about to do, what she was, in fact, already doing. She had raised the bone, and was tearing at it with her teeth, spasmodically chewing, swallowing by great gulps which her throat threatened to return. But did not. She flung the bone away only after it was cleaned, and followed slowly*

in the wake of her cannibal mentors ... But there remained what amounted to an abomination of human behaviour, a headache, and the first signs of indigestion. In the light of Christian morality she must never think of the incident again.

The tasting of human flesh is described as feeding her spirit. Cannibalism connects Ellen to the primordial and savage part of the self that Western culture has repressed.

Academic Veronica Brady observes that *A Fringe of Leaves* is not about the Aboriginal people, but rather about being non-Aboriginal in Australia and the unease that Australians need to settle as they build a nation. For Patrick White, Aboriginal people are representations of the repressed parts of the European self, symbols for the repressed white psyche.

... Aboriginal people are representations of the repressed parts of the European self ...

Sigmund Freud would have interpreted Ellen's act as representing her assimilation with the land and its Aboriginal custodians. Freud hypothesised that cannibalistic narratives represented desire. For example, erotic desire was seen as an all-consuming passion, one that seeks assimilation with the object of lust. In his book

Totem and Taboo: Some Points of Agreement between the Mental Lives of Savages and Neurotics he writes of the Aboriginal people in Australia. He refers to them as 'naked cannibals', 'the most backward and miserable' of savages, and claims that the motive for cannibalism among the 'primitive races' is the belief that the characteristics of the person consumed become part of the person who eats them – the ultimate consumption of 'the other'.

CANNIBALISM IN EUROPEAN CULTURE

While psychoanalysis gives us one way to try to understand the European fascination with cannibalism, there is another reason why Captain Fraser expected to find cannibals everywhere. European accounts of man-eating practices have a rich history, passed down through mythology, folklore and fairytales. These have left a legacy that continues to pervade the contemporary imagination – from *Dracula* to *Silence of the Lambs* – with the spectre of cannibalism as one of the darkest of acts.

Fairytales told to children before bedtime are riddled with cannibalistic themes: a witch in *Hansel and Gretel* attempts to lure two children into an oven; a giant in *Jack and the Beanstalk* thunders, 'Be he alive or be he dead, I'll grind his bones to make my bread'; a wicked stepmother in *Sleeping Beauty* feeds a stew to her husband that she believes has her stepdaughter's heart in it.

Although the term was common in the colonial context, the use of the word 'cannibal' to denigrate those who were different had already had a long history on the European continent. The label was attached to anyone who was perceived as dangerous or culturally or ethnically 'other'. Anthropologist William Arens notes that the suggestion that early Christians may have been cannibals is now assumed to have been false. In a similar vein, centuries-long charges by Christians that Jews resorted to this practice are now 'a source of embarrassment to liberal thinkers'.

The Romans accused the Christians of using blood in mysterious secret rites, perhaps derived from a misunderstanding about the nature of the Eucharist. In an example of how the claim was then used against the Jews, historian Reay Tannahill writes of an incident in 1401 where a man living in Diessenhofen, Switzerland, murdered a four-year-old boy and, under torture, confessed that he had promised to sell the boy's blood to a Jewish visitor from Schaffhausen. The visitor and all the Jews of Diessenhofen were burned – as were many of the Jews of Schaffhausen.

In the sixteenth and seventeenth centuries, witches attracted accusations of cannibalism. Midwives were especially vulnerable to accusations of witchcraft and cannibalism since they were seen as having ready access to a supply of (unbaptised) babies. If children died, their deaths were often attributed to the devil's work, with their dead bodies used in the making of potions, brews and pies.

While Jews, Christians and wayward women may have had accusations of cannibalism levelled at them as proof of their connection to the devil, there have also been many notorious accounts of cannibalism committed as acts of tyranny or madness, especially in gothic literature and in folklore. Vlad V of Walachia – or Vlad the Impaler, muse of the vampire genre – was said to have beheaded his foes, allowed crabs to feast upon them and then fed the crabs to his victims' friends and relatives. From Edgar Allen Poe's *Narrative of A Gordon Pym* to Fyodor Dostoyevsky's dark comic reflections in *The Idiot*, people pushed to the extremes have resorted to cannibalism and the act has become a symbol of lost humanity.

It is no surprise then that cannibalism features prominently in the most famous story in which a man survives in the most solitary and uncivilised of conditions.

ROBINSON CRUSOE: THE DREAD OF FALLING INTO THE HANDS OF SAVAGES AND CANNIBALS

Daniel Defoe was an English writer, journalist and spy, and one of the founders of the English novel. He was a prolific writer, penning over 500 books, pamphlets and journals on topics including politics, crime, religion, marriage, psychology and the supernatural. But it is his novel *Robinson Crusoe*, published in 1719, which became an enduring classic.

Robinson Crusoe, an adventurer with recurring bad luck, is shipwrecked while trying his hand at the slave trade. He is the sole survivor, washed ashore on a deserted island where he has to live in a 'State of Nature' to survive.

He uses what he finds on the island and salvages from shipwrecks to stay alive and develop his own fiefdom on the land.

During his time at sea, before the shipwreck, Crusoe assumes that cannibals inhabit the shores he sails past. He lives with the fear that 'where we could ne'er once go on shoar but we should be devour'd by savage Beasts'. Now stranded, he lives in the shadow of fear.

Defoe's narrative is not simply one of tall-tale adventure. It is also a spiritual biography, a religious allegory in the spirit of John Bunyan's *The Pilgrim's Progress*. Crusoe is a physical and spiritual castaway. With missionary undertones, his story is one of rebellion, punishment (for irreligion and for disobeying his parents), repentance and deliverance. During his solitary time on the island, Crusoe has time for reflection and undergoes spiritual conversion. He comes to view his situation as one that allows him to find and commune with God.

Crusoe's proprietorship over the island that he is living on comes quickly. The island is established as his domain so that he – the outsider – becomes the 'owner' and the savages, who have long been visiting the island, become the intruders. He works the soil in the Hobbesian manner and it is therefore his. While the savages come and go, proving they have no permanent attachment to the land, Crusoe uses the land productively, keeping the threatening savages at bay with his overwhelming firearm power. Against this force, the savages just fade away – disappear. But after five years of solitary living, Crusoe comes across a 'Print of a Man's naked Foot on the Shore', a reminder of the danger of the savages to which he is becoming complacent. His fears are renewed.

Crusoe later discovers that the dreaded cannibals are regular visitors to the island, landing on the side away from where he has established himself. They use the island to partake of cannibalistic feasts that resemble and evoke Spanish depictions of bloody orgies. These were based on the beliefs of Defoe's contemporaries as to how cannibalistic rituals were performed in these godforsaken parts of the world. Crusoe comes across the aftermath of one such event. The scene, filled with 'the Horror of the Degeneracy of Humane Nature' creates physical and spiritual revulsion in Crusoe. He gives thanks to God that he was 'distinguish'd from such dreadful Creatures as these'.

His initial reaction to the cannibals is a fear that generates genocidal fantasies. Even in his subconscious he 'dream'd often of killing the Savages'. After much reflection, and reasoning that any aggression by him may be met with reprisals, Crusoe comes to realise that this savagery is not *their* fault; they know no better. Indeed, he decides, the cannibals can be saved. Just as Crusoe has received redemption from God, so too can the cannibals.

Religion joyn'd in with this Prudential, and I was convinc'd now many Ways, that I was perfectly out of my Duty, when I was laying all my bloody Schemes for the Destruction of innocent Creatures, I mean

innocent as to me ... and I ought to leave them to the
Justice of God ...

There is an incident, during Crusoe's twenty-third year of solitude, when cannibals arrive on his side of the island and he is greeted with another scene of bloodlust and carnage:

> *This was a dreadful Sight to me, especially when going down to the Shore. I could see the marks of Horror, which the dismal Work they had been about had left behind it, <u>viz.</u> The Blood, the Bones, and part of the Flesh of humane Bodies, eaten and devour'd by those Wretches ... I began now to premeditate the Destruction of the next that I saw there, let them be who, or hoe many soever.*

'The Blood, the Bones, the part of the Flesh of humane Bodies, eaten and devour'd ... '

During his revulsions, and in keeping with the ideologies of Defoe's time, Crusoe perceives that despite their barbarity, the savages are useful for labour (but labour only), and Crusoe intends to save them for Christianising and subservience. During his twenty-fifth year of solitude, Crusoe realises his dream of taking a savage as a slave.

He saves a would-be victim – 'his' man Friday – and gets eternal servitude in return.

To the modern reader, Crusoe's power is evident in his ability to name: he calls his servant 'Friday' and gives himself the title of 'Master'. Crusoe's mastery over Friday is portrayed as one of kindly Christian benevolence.

> ... [he] made all the Signs to me of Subjection, Servitude, and Submission imaginable, to let me know, how he would serve me as long as he liv'd ... I began to speak to him, and teach him to speak to me; and first I made him know his Name should be <u>Friday</u>, which was the Day I sav'd his Life; I call'd him so for the Memory of the Time; I likewise taught him to say <u>Master</u>.

Having physically saved Friday, Crusoe now sets about attaining his servant's spiritual redemption. The first way to do this is to cure Friday of the most obvious sign of his irreligion – his barbaric lust for human flesh, his cannibalistic tendencies. This proves a challenge and Friday, like a child, needs to be socialised.

> I caus'd Friday to gather all the Skulls, Bones, Flesh, and whatever remain'd, and lay them together on a Heap, and make a great Fire upon it, and burn them all to Ashes: I found Friday had still a hankering Stomach after some of the Flesh, and was still a Cannibal in his Nature; but I discover'd so much

Abhorrence at the very Thoughts of it, and at the least Appearance of it, that he durst not discover it; for I had by some Means let him know, that I would kill him if he offer'd it.

Crusoe's plan is to give Friday a taste of goat's meat – and this does the trick. Liberated from this most obvious mark of barbarity, Crusoe sets out to Christianise Friday, Crusoe playing the role of 'saviour' to 'the savage'. He physically rescues Friday from the other cannibals, and rescues him morally and spiritually by delivering him up to the Lord.

When the savages arrive with a European, Crusoe cannot sit idly by. He shoots them in 'the Name of God' – a justification for his own genocidal barbarity – and frees the Spanish castaways. Eventual rescue from the island sees Friday continue as Crusoe's valet.

In *Émile*, Jean-Jacques Rousseau instructs his young charge that there is only one book that provides a 'complete treatise on natural education' – *Robinson Crusoe*:

It will be the text to which all our talks about natural science are but the commentary. It will serve to test our progress towards a right judgement, and it will always be read with delight, so long as our taste is unspoilt … The surest way to raise him above prejudice and to base his judgements on the true relations of things, is to put him in the place of a solitary man, and to judge all things as they would be judged by such a man in relation to their own utility.

Rousseau's idea of 'natural education' and those who romanticise the idea of a noble savage and a 'State of Nature' seem to overlook that in *Robinson Crusoe* the savages are just another obstacle to survival; that they are cannibals only adds to the danger.

This 'State of Nature' is deceptive for, unlike the Caribs (Crusoe's 'cannibals'), who would have been able to survive in the environment, Crusoe builds up a 'civilization of comfort' mostly from European technology salvaged from the shipwrecks. His attitude is that of an imperialist capitalist. Everywhere he finds things he can conquer – nature, land and men – and sets about exploiting the resources of his environment. The jungle is tamed by the technology of the European, and Friday is in fearful awe of the firing of a gun. Crusoe's power over the native is because of the superiority of his weapons, not, as he claims, the 'endorsement of God'.

Literary theorist and academic John Thieme observes that Defoe's novel can be read as a 'blueprint for colonialism' and Crusoe effectively develops a plantation economy 'staffed by a one-man subservient labour force in the form of Man Friday'. It is a story that encapsulates the ideologies that would shape colonisation: the inferiority and barbarity of the savages, the superiority of the whites as evidenced by their advanced technology, the need to tame the barbarity of the savages, the use of tamed savages as a pool of labour and the toiling of the land to prove proprietorship over it.

Tales such as *Robinson Crusoe* horrified European

readers and listeners with its portrayal of those who peopled the non-European points of the globe as barbaric. This construction of indigenous peoples as cannibalistic reinforced the need for their civilising, controlling and conquering, and was used to justify the excessive force and brutality of colonisation, as well as to highlight the need to spread Christianity to these dark parts of the world. It is a story that says that the barbarity of the savages (cannibalism) justifies the violence against them (genocide).

Robinson Crusoe was an enormously popular novel for centuries. It would have shaped its readers' views on both the undiscovered parts of the planet and the people who lived there. But its enduring resonance for readers would also indicate that it tapped into something in the public consciousness that readers could relate to. Certainly in *Robinson Crusoe* there is an echo of the message in John Curtis's version of Eliza Fraser's adventures – that by bringing Christianity to them, the cannibals will turn away from their barbaric nature.

CANNIBALISM AND COLONISATION

While there are many reasons for the colonial European obsession with cannibalism, the impact of the label on those accused of such barbarity was hardly inconsequential. The brutal Spanish conquest of South America shows the greatest hostility towards those, like the Caribs, who resisted Spanish colonisation. 'Cannibals' became synonymous with the imputed savagery of the indigenous habitants and was used to justify the ruthless force with which they were dealt.

Another important aspect to the label of 'cannibal' was that the Spanish were, under their laws, allowed to capture only cannibals for the slave trade. This economic advantage ensured that the term was applied liberally. Claims of cannibalism became more prominent as colonisation (along with all its own barbarities) had to be justified. At the same time, the practice was claimed to have disappeared in the face of European presence, a triumph for civilisation and Christianity.

Throughout the 1700s and 1800s, stories of cannibalism circulated among sailors and travellers on the frontier, adding a certain tension to the expectations of those who ventured into the blank spaces on the maps. Such tales worked best when an area remained unexplored and unknown to Europeans. The empty patches held the darkest customs of the darkest peoples.

Western travellers on the fringes of the European empires, in places of early contact, brought back stories of native cannibalism. Explorers and seafarers too were seen as sources of information about the cannibals who populated foreign lands. Indeed, sailors – like Captain Fraser and his crew – expected to find the practice at the outposts of European expansion and they had a pathological fear of it.

While Spanish colonists brought back tales of cannibalistic feasts, there were some who tried to understand these practices in context, presenting the situation as a cross-cultural conflict.

French Renaissance philosopher Michel de Montaigne in his essay 'On Cannibalism' asserts that the barbarism of the so-called savages was no worse than the barbarism of Europeans. Unlike Jean-Jacques Rousseau, who saw the wildness of the natives as noble, natural and innocent, Montaigne believed that while natives were cruel and barbaric, this was a characteristic they shared with Europeans:

> *It does not sadden me that we should note the horrible barbarity in a practice such as theirs: what does sadden me is that, while judging correctly of their wrong-doings, we should be so blind to our own. I think there is more barbarity in eating a man alive than in eating him dead; more barbarity in lacerating by rack and torture a body still fully able to feel things, in roasting him little by little and having him bruised and bitten by pigs and dogs (as we have not only read about but seen in recent memory, not among enemies in antiquity but among fellow-citizens and neighbours – and, what is worse, in the name of duty and religion) than in roasting him and eating him after his death.*

There is a split in the pre-1980s literature on the practice of cannibalism. On the one hand, there are those who see the practice as evidence of a depraved, barbarous society and nature and who usually characterise cannibalistic acts as the execution of bloodlust. On the other hand, there are those, like French scholar Frank Lestringant, who seek to justify the acts of cannibalism by trying to adopt a non-Eurocentric approach, characterising cannibalism as nutritional or ritualistic:

> *Perhaps they did happen to eat human flesh occasionally, but nobody is perfect – and they did at least eat it cooked, and confined themselves to the flesh of their enemies.*

The tension between these approaches towards cannibalism underwent a fundamental shift with the publication of anthropologist William Arens's *The Man-Eating Myth* in 1979. Arens observes that 'cannibal' is a label that at one time or another has been applied to every human group. He asserts that as there are no verifiable eyewitness accounts of the practice, we must be sceptical of its existence. His suspicions were raised by the pattern of cannibalism so quickly disappearing the minute anthropologists arrived, as though contact with Western civilisation had resulted in the custom's immediate demise even if it was the only trait that was abandoned by indigenous people so easily. He concludes that the evidence is insufficient to justify either the label of 'cannibal' or the assumption that the practice occurred before the arrival of the Europeans.

Scholars such as William Arens and, later, Gananath Obeyesekere have concluded that virtually no evidence can be found to support the widespread Western belief that the peoples on the fringes of the Empire were cannibals. Arens even challenges the research of Nobel Prize winner Daniel Carleton Gajdusek on the 'cannibals' of New Guinea. (Gajdusek claims that cannibalism is conclusively proven by its connection to the mysterious disease kuru.)

The indigenous people of New Guinea, Fiji, Brazil and the Caribbean have all been subjected to anthropological claims that they were 'cannibals'. But upon investigation it can be seen that initial claims of the practice were exaggerated or fantasised, and that anthropologists brought cultural baggage into these first-contact zones.

Evidence of cannibalism in first-contact experiences and second-hand accounts is suspect because of the cultural and racial lens of the viewer, whose expectations and assumptions lead them to interpret what they see according to what they expect to find. In these circumstances, the flimsiest evidence is taken as proof. Often reliance is made on seafaring yarns, an obviously unreliable and unscientific approach in any discipline, and many imaginative assumptions have been made about the discovery of unidentifiable bones. Yet these accounts have often been relied upon by anthropologists and other experts in their academic writing.

Since Arens's deconstruction and exposé of the canonical material, the debate surrounding cannibalistic practices has shifted. The legacy of scholars such as Arens has been that anthropologists and cultural studies theorists are more sceptical of such claims. Arens does not conclude that there was no cannibalism (a claim often attributed to him); rather he takes the question of whether or not people ate each other as 'interesting but moot'. He muses that 'if the idea that they do is commonly accepted without adequate documentation, then the reason for this state of affairs is an even more intriguing problem', though he is 'dubious about the actual existence of this act as an accepted practice for any time or place'.

For Arens and like-minded scholars, the important question is not what this obsession with the alleged cannibals tells us about the colonised, but what it reveals about the colonisers who were so fascinated with cannibalism. As literature professor Peter Hulme writes:

> ... *why were Europeans so desirous of finding confirmation of their suspicions of cannibalism? And why does cannibalism feature so insistently as a contemporary trope in different forms of writing?*

CANNIBALISM IN AUSTRALIA

Just as Crusoe thought he saw cannibals everywhere and Captain Fraser assumed that the inhabitants of the lands he sailed past were filled with them, early colonists in Australia presumed the same thing. Consider this extract from Curtis's account:

> *Too many instances have occurred to doubt that cannibalism is practised among many of the Australian tribes, and in a manner the most revolting; not only their enemies slain in war, and those unfortunate Europeans who have fallen into their power, have been eaten, but numerous examples have occurred, of the father killing and eating his own offspring! Hunger long continued – intense ravening hunger, is the excuse made for such barbarism. So vitiated is their taste, that they have been known to bleed themselves, in order to make a sort of cake of blood, which they greedily devour!*

The assumption that Aborigines were cannibals was also evident in the journals of European travellers. Charles Sturt can provide just one example. Sturt was an English explorer, born in British India, educated in England and later part of a regiment that escorted convicts to New South Wales. He first came to Australia in 1827 and subsequently led several expeditions into the interior of Australia, starting from both Sydney and later Adelaide. His expeditions traced several of the westward-flowing rivers, establishing that they all merge into the Murray River, thereby dispelling the theory that there was an inland sea.

During his tour of the Murrumbidgee in 1829, he observes:

> *He was, however, sacrificed; and both the men were eaten by the tribe generally. I questioned several on the subject, but they preserved the most sullen silence, neither acknowledging nor denying the fact.*

Sturt takes this silence as assent and that becomes his best evidence. Sturt also records cannibalistic infanticide:

> *'That fellow, sir', said he, 'who is sitting down, killed his infant child last night by knocking its head against a stone, after which he threw it in the fire and devoured it' ... I therefore went up to the man and questioned him as to the fact as well as I could. He did not attempt to deny it, but slunk away in evident consciousness. I then questioned the other that remained, whose excuse for his friend was that the child was sick and would never have grown up, adding that he himself did not patter (eat) any of it.*

Again, it is assumption, hearsay and the lack of direct refutation that provide Sturt with his evidence. He becomes obsessed with his subject, writing:

> *I am myself, however, as firmly persuaded of the truth of what I have stated as if I had seen the savage commit the act ... the very mention of such a thing*

among these people goes to prove they are capable of such enormity.

Among Cannibals: An Account of Four Years' Travels in Australia and of Camp Life with the Aborigines of Queensland was written by explorer and ethnographer Carl Lumholtz in 1889. Lumholtz was a member of the Royal Society of Sciences of Norway and he was in no doubt about the cannibalism of the Aboriginal people he encountered around the Herbert River:

> *The Australians are cannibals. A fallen foe, be it man, woman or child, is eaten as the choicest delicacy; they know no greater luxury than the flesh of a black man.*

Lumholtz believed the Aboriginal people to be inherently treacherous and untrustworthy.

> *When he talked he rubbed his belly with complacency, as if the sight of me made his mouth water, and he gave me an impression that he would like to devour me on the spot. He always wore a smiling face, a mask behind which all the natives conceal their treacherous nature …*

> *I afterwards learned that he was a cunning fellow, and was successful in procuring human flesh, and there is nothing else that ensures respect among the Australian aborigines in so high a degree.*

Despite describing himself as someone who was sympathetic towards Aboriginal people, he saw them as a doomed race.

> *The philanthropist is filled with sadness when he sees the original inhabitants of this strange land succumbing according to the inexorable law of degeneration. Invading civilization has not brought development and progress to the Australian native; after a few generations his race will have disappeared from the face of the earth.*

Prospector and explorer HGB Mason's book *Darkest Western Australia* was published in 1909. According to him:

> *These male Aboriginals are all cannibals. The height of a nigger's ambition is to kill and eat some member of another tribe; although quite content to eat his own off-spring or barter them for weapons of exceptional value. When the children are considered fat enough the killing is not delayed.*

And:

> *The child is roasted in the same manner as an emu or kangaroo. The bucks present sit around the fire unconcernedly, pretending to sharpen and polish their spears and other weapons; though with an*

intense longing in their gleaming eyes. This is the happiest moment in their lives. The lust for flesh, once having been tasted by a nigger, is only equalled by a man-eating tiger, of the two the more cleanly and graceful animal.

Another well-known 'source' of cannibalistic accounts was anthropologist Daisy Bates. Bates lived among various Aboriginal communities, including Ooldea, where she

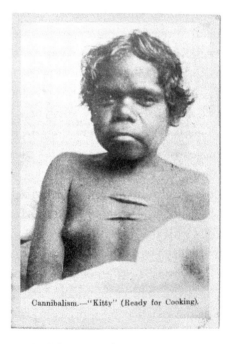

Cannibalism.—"Kitty" (Ready for Cooking).

Despite a lack of concrete evidence, accusations of cannibalism were levelled at Aboriginal people. *(Image by HGB Mason, published in* Darkest Western Australia*)*

remained for sixteen years, dressed in her long dark skirts and high collars, sheltering under her parasol. In her book *The Native Tribes of Western Australia*, she on occasion refers to her Aboriginal contacts as 'cannibals' in the ordinary course of her descriptions.

For all her time living among Aboriginal people, Bates had fairly intolerant views. She believed that Aboriginal people were a dying race and she disliked 'half-castes'. Historian Bob Reece, in his biography *Daisy Bates: Grand Dame of the Desert*, admires her determination and her role as a self-taught female anthropologist but concludes she was also 'a social climber, name-dropper and user of people, a diehard imperial loyalist and an apologist for the Western Australian pastoralists in their treatment of the Aborigines'. The work of people like Daisy Bates has subsequently been described as sensationalised and stereotyped, using little reliable direct evidence, hampered by imperfect knowledge of the languages of those involved, and reliant on the hearsay of informants, both white and black.

Archaeologist and anthropologist Michael Pickering argues in his doctoral thesis, 'Cannibalism among Aborigines: A Critical Review of the Literary Evidence', that authors who have looked at the incidences of cannibalism in Australia have neglected to consider the accuracy of, or circumstances behind, their sources. Many assessments of the practice are more concerned with the nature of the practice than its actual existence. He adds that recent researchers writing on cannibalism have largely neglected evaluating the reliability of their primary data, confusing observational and anecdotal data.

Pickering's carefully considered conclusion is that for most groups it was certainly never practised and was seen as socially unacceptable behaviour. As to any doubts, 'it appears … though the evidence is not conclusive, that the consumption of human flesh was, in some areas' – Pickering speculates that this may have been areas of north-eastern Queensland, coastal Arnhem Land, and parts of Victoria – 'a socially sanctioned and controlled, though still rare and infrequent, practice, but it is difficult to accurately establish by which groups'.

He concludes that, quantitatively speaking, there is no evidence to prove cannibalism was practised anywhere in Australia, and it would be unjustified, given the unreliability of most evidence, to attempt to identify specific groups by name.

Most claims of cannibalism, according to Pickering, stem from totally unsubstantiated and usually conjectural statements that have 'fed' one another over time, thus perpetuating as well as perpetrating, both intentionally and unintentionally, exaggerated accounts of the frequency, form and nature of cannibalism by Aboriginal people. It is likely that many observers misunderstood what they were viewing and made assumptions about the acts they witnessed, and possibly mistook metaphorical allusions for literal acts.

Nevertheless, the assumptions that anthropologists confirmed with their reliance on questionable evidence permeated popular culture.

The Bulletin developed a comic cannibal, accompanied by cartoon stereotypes of dark natives in loincloths and large pieces of jewellery. This image was often used to poke fun at the missionaries trying to Christianise heathens. An illustration in *The Bulletin* titled 'Faithful beyond Death – The Story of a Missionary in Three Chapters' shows a pious missionary, then a thin 'native' with the caption 'The Reception Committee'. A third illustration depicts a fattened 'native', two boots clearly protruding from his stomach with the caption 'Voice from Within: "My friend, you have forgotten to say grace".'

A short story published in *The Bulletin* in 1895 titled 'A Black Heathen' begins: 'Topknot was a nigger with a bad reputation.' It chronicles the close encounter a white man named Ogilvie has when thwarting Topknot's attempt to feast upon his flesh. 'Do you know what he told me he was going to do? … First of all cut that piece out of my breast and eat it in front of me.'

All this might be very entertaining and amusing to the reader – and the brunt of the joke is not so much the 'native' as the pious missionary seeking to convert those whose ways are intractable. But the result is that 'Aboriginal' and 'savage', 'nigger' and 'cannibal' are often used interchangeably.

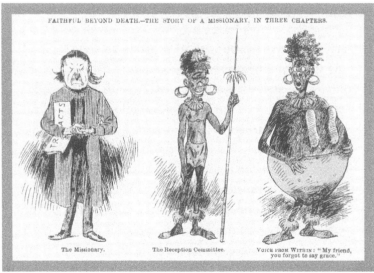

The 'Topknot' and 'Faithful beyond Death' cartoons from *The Bulletin* exemplify the way in which images of cannibals entered Australian popular culture. *(Courtesy of Bauer Media)*

Actual accounts of cannibalism by Aboriginal people are sketchy at best, and the most reliable documentary evidence does not record cannibalism by blacks but by whites. Cannibalism was always claimed to have occurred on the frontiers of European 'civilisation', in places where white people felt most vulnerable and their ability to survive seemed most precarious. Accounts of cannibalism circulated during times of hardship and famine: Ireland between 1588 and 1589 and between 1601 and 1603, in France in 1594 when Henri IV besieged Paris, and during the 900-day siege of Leningrad in World War II.

The particular and precarious vulnerability felt on the frontier often brought out the worst in colonising Europeans. Alexander Pearce was the only survivor of a party of seven (some accounts put it at eight) convict runaways from Macquarie Harbour who had successively killed and eaten each other in 1822. With his usual flair, Robert Hughes in *The Fatal Shore* describes him as 'a little, pockmarked, blue-eyed Irishman from County Monaghan who had been transported for seven years at the Armagh Assizes in 1819, for stealing six pairs of shoes'. Pearce was not executed but instead sent back to Macquarie Harbour. In 1823 he absconded a second time and upon recapture confessed to having murdered and eaten his fellow escapee, Thomas Cox. A piece of human flesh, about half a pound, was found in his pocket. Pearce confessed all the particulars of the murder and then offered to show where he had left Cox's remains. As Hughes writes:

… Cox's body lay 'in a dreadfully mangled state', according to one official report, being cut right through the middle, the head off, the privates torn off, all the flesh off the calves of the legs, back of the thighs and loins, also off the thick part of the arms, which the inhuman wretch declared was the most delicious of food.

Pearce had been gone only five days from the settlement. He claimed that he had killed Cox in self-defence but was charged and convicted of murder and hanged. The court ordered that Pearce should be 'disjointed' after death and delivered to the surgeons. His head was given to an American phrenologist, Dr Samuel Morton, who had a collection of skulls and shrunken heads. Pearce became a figure of folklore and was the inspiration for the character Matt Gabbett in Marcus Clarke's *For the Term of His Natural Life*.

In another instance, the convicts Edward Broughton and Mathew Maccavoy were hanged in 1832 'for the wilful Murder of three of their Fellow Transports and eating them as Food'.

Cannibalism between escaped convicts was treated as murder but there was a time when cannibalism was an accepted custom by sailors lost at sea. It was deemed necessary when starving and shipwrecked to eat someone so that others might live, as selected by the drawing of 'lots' or straws.

The English courts in the 1884 case of *R v. Dudley and*

Stephens considered the practice of cannibalism among castaways. This case highlighted the tension between seafaring protocol during a crisis ('the custom of the sea') and the middle-class horror of the act of cannibalism.

In July 1884, Tom Dudley, Edwin Stephens, Ned Brooks and Richard Parker set sail to Sydney on the *Mignonette*. The yacht was wrecked in a storm as it started its turn around the Cape of Good Hope and the crew abandoned ship for an open boat. They floated for twenty days with no food or fresh water except for two cans of turnips and a turtle they had managed to catch. When Parker became seriously ill, Dudley and Stephens, without Brooks's or Parker's consent, agreed to kill Parker, who was only young, had no dependants and was dying anyway. Parker, in serious ill-health, offered no resistance to being killed but did not agree to it either. Dudley, Stephens and Brooks fed on his blood and flesh before being picked up by a passing vessel on the twenty-fourth day of their ordeal. If they had not fed on Parker they would have died.

That Captain Dudley believed he had acted according to accepted custom is shown by the way in which he freely admitted to the act. No attempt was made to conceal the events that had taken place, and upon his arrival in Falmouth, Dudley produced eight copies of his account, including one for the Home Office, written in order to explain the loss of the yacht to its owner.

Dudley believed that he had to account for the boat but that he had not broken the law in the measures he had taken to stay alive. As he saw it, a formal inquiry would have been a mere formality to get an official seal of approval for his conduct so that he could be set free, judicially exonerated from any blame in the matter.

Legal historian AW Brian Simpson in *Cannibalism and the Common Law* notes that the practice was so normal 'that on some occasions survivors found it appropriate to take pains to *volunteer* denial that cannibalism had occurred'. Suspicion of cannibalism among starving castaways was a routine reaction, so it was not surprising that Captain Dudley assumed he had acted in an acceptable manner under the circumstances. Even if the folklore about cannibalism was inaccurate or pure myth, Simpson writes:

> *… it is quite clear that the situation confronting the survivors of the yacht <u>Mignonette</u> was one for which they were well prepared and that in a general sense, Dudley and his companions knew the proper thing to do … They knew too the appropriate preliminary course of action, which was to draw lots, a practice viewed as legitimating killing and cannibalism, particularly if agreed upon by a council of sailors.*

R v. Dudley and Stephens was a test case about the legality of the 'custom of the sea'. Charges against Brooks were dropped by the Home Office. There was strong public support for the accused and the decision to set them free on bail pending trial was met with public applause from the local crowd. The press initially condemned their actions and said they should be brought to trial, but as the proceedings commenced and concluded, there was increased support for a pardon.

Public sympathy escalated with the publication of a letter written by Dudley to his wife, penned at a time when he thought it would be his last. Popular support, including the raising of funds for the sailors' families and legal defence, was predominantly from the working class, especially from those whose work was linked to the sea and who appreciated how perilous such a livelihood was. The general consensus from this sector of the community was that the act, although morally indefensible, did not merit punishment. But there was upper-class condemnation of the act.

In considering whether acts of necessity were a defence to the crime of murder, as was the case in self-defence or acts of war, Chief Justice Lord Coleridge noted that hunger was no excuse for larceny, nor was it an excuse for murder. In the present circumstances, the court held that '[t]o preserve one's life is generally speaking a duty, but it may be the plainest and highest duty to sacrifice it'. And later in the judgement: 'But a man has no right to declare temptation to be an excuse, though he might himself have yielded to it …' Thus the conclusion was that the facts showed the threat of starvation was no defence to murder.

Coleridge's judgement seems cautious in not providing an excuse for crime through the defence of necessity as though to admit such a thing would be to allow extreme temptation to exculpate individuals from criminal liability. He attempts to articulate morally correct standards of behaviour, even if they are difficult to follow:

It must not be supposed that in refusing to admit temptation to be an excuse for crime it is forgotten how terrible the temptation was, how awful the suffering; how hard in such trials to keep the judgement straight and the conduct pure. We are often compelled to set up standards we cannot reach ourselves, and to lay down rules which we ourselves could not satisfy.

However, more was at stake than just the fear of opening up defences to murder on the basis of need. If British sailors showed the same willingness to consume flesh as it was imagined uncivilised peoples of the world did, it would seem that white civilisation was much closer to primitive society than had been constructed. A sentence of death was passed on the defendants but was later commuted to six months in prison. Tom Dudley, innocent in his own eyes, was released in 1885, a year and a day after the *Mignonette* had set sail on its fateful voyage. He emigrated to Australia that same year.

CANNIBALISM AMONG THE COLONISERS

When Captain Fraser found himself shipwrecked off the coast of Australia, cannibalism was a product of British behaviour and fantasies. Escaped convicts and ship-wrecked sailors engaged in cannibalism when they were struggling to survive inhospitable and fraught situations. But in such circumstances, it was an act of desperation reviled because it showed the capacity of Europeans, who considered themselves to be the most civilised of peoples, to behave in a way that they believed to be quintessentially primitive.

While instances such as Alexander Pearce were dismissed as 'exceptional' – which indeed they were – there was no restraint in labelling Aboriginal people as 'cannibals' based on colonial prejudices rather than evidence. A distinction was drawn between cannibalism as a desperate act of survival to fend off starvation (practised by whites) and cannibalism as evidence of a barbaric nature and culture (purportedly practised by blacks).

The label of 'cannibal' made Aboriginal people appear less human and justified their subordination, and their supposed savagery was also used as a rationalisation for denying Aboriginal rights, for taking and occupying Aboriginal land, and for destroying Aboriginal culture. The label camouflaged the atrocities on the frontier committed against Aboriginal people and reinforced racist stereotypes about them. As Inga Clendinnen observed in her 1999 Boyer Lecture: 'White men really do need mirrors.'

Others have noted the irony of calling the natives 'cannibals' when the act of colonisation could itself be embodied in a metaphor of cannibalism. Karl Marx observed that capitalism itself was a form of cannibalism: 'Capital is dead labour which, vampire-like, lives only by sucking living labour, and lives the more, the more labour it sucks.'

Perhaps the last word should go to Jonathan Swift's 'Modest Proposal', published anonymously in 1729, in which he parodied colonial callousness and the inhuman rationale of market economics by proposing that the children of Irish poor be eaten by the rich:

And, it is exactly at one Year old, that I propose to provide for them in such a Manner, as instead of being a Charge upon their Parents, or the Parish, or wanting Food and Raiment for the rest of their Lives; they shall, on the contrary, contribute to the Feeding, and partly to the Clothing, of many Thousands … I HAVE been assured by a very knowing American of my Acquaintance in London, that a young healthy Child well nurs'd, is, at a Year old, a most delicious, nourishing, and wholesome Food; whether Stewed, Roasted, Baked, or Boiled; and I make no doubt that it will equally serve in a Fricassée, or a Ragoût … A Child will make two Dishes at an Entertainment for Friends; and when the Family dines alone, the fore or hind Quarter will make a reasonable Dish; and seasoned with a little Pepper or Salt, will be very good Boiled on the fourth Day, especially in Winter.

Swift equated this cannibalism of the flesh with the cannibalistic nature of colonial imperialism that saw the Irish become so destitute.

> *I GRANT this Food will be somewhat dear, and therefore very <u>proper for Landlords</u>; who, as they have already devoured most of the Parents, seem to have the best Title to the Children.*

He claimed his proposal would reduce Irish dependency and poverty and justified his suggestion by using the rationale of market:

> *I HAVE already computed the Charge of nursing a Beggar's Child (in which List I reckon all <u>Cottagers</u>, <u>Labourers</u>, and Four fifths of the <u>Farmers</u>) to be about two Shillings per annum, Rags included; and I believe, no Gentleman would repine to give Ten Shillings for the <u>Carcase of a good fat Child</u>; which, as I have said, will make four Dishes of excellent nutritive Meat, when he hath only some particular Friend, or his own Family, to dine with him. Thus the Squire will learn to be a good Landlord, and grow popular among his Tenants; the Mother will have Eight Shillings net Profit, and be fit for Work until she produceth another Child. THOSE who are more thrifty (<u>as I must confess the Times require</u>) may flay the Carcase; the Skin of which, artificially*

dressed, will make admirable Gloves for Ladies, and Summer Boots for fine Gentlemen.

Swift's political satire was aimed at the English politicians and Irish landlords who kept the Irish in a state of poverty and then complained that they were beggars and thieves. His proposal, Swift concluded, would solve the economic, social and gastronomical problems of Ireland in one fell swoop. Swift clearly understood that the metaphor of cannibalism more easily applied to the behaviour of the dominant than the weak, describing the behaviour of the coloniser more accurately than that of the colonised.

7

Imagining Noble Savages

ELIZA'S BLACKS WERE treacherous cannibals. Her Aboriginal women were mean, petty and jealous. Negative stereotypes pervaded her story both in terms of the character of Aboriginal people and their cultural practices.

It's not difficult to spot a negative stereotype, especially when looking back to another time when theories of white racial superiority were far more acceptable and pervasive. The obviously negative images of cruel, barbaric savages are easy targets of our critique today. But contemporary fascination with Aboriginal culture – and a sympathy for Aboriginal people – has led not only to an interest in but also a romanticism of Aboriginal culture, as well as a reverence for the ideal of the noble savage, which portrays Aboriginal people as mythical, super-wise, super-human figures.

The noble savage is, of course, not a recent invention. The concept is often associated with Jean-Jacques Rousseau even though he never used the phrase. It first appears in 1672 in *The Conquest of Granada*, a play by John Dryden:

I am as free as nature first made man,
Ere the base laws of servitude began,
When wild in woods the noble savage ran.

The concept continues to find modern reiterations. Take the following example from *Wonderful Australia in Pictures*, published by the Herald & Weekly Times in 1949, where the noble-savage ideal persists in representations of the 'Aboriginal character':

Such are the Australians – the original Australians. A kindly, gentle and patient people, they are heirs to an ancient culture which the white takes from them, giving nothing in return. They are self-reliant, observant (their fame as trackers is notable and deserved), frank, open and fond of laughter. And lest we think of the Aborigine as a lower form of life, it is well to remember that, as Dr W Ramsey Smith says, 'his morality is as high as among the generality of white, uneducated people.' Indeed, it may well be said that it is in some respects even higher.

The above passage is not describing an Aboriginal person who lives in a contemporary Aboriginal community but one who lives in pre-contact society, the 'ancient culture', an Aborigine who lives in the past. The primitive state they remain in makes them a subject of curiosity:

*In many respects the aboriginal natives are the most
astonishing of all Australia's curiosities, for in the
atomic age of man's greatest discoveries this lost race
remains in an apparent state of arrested development,
held like living fossils in the museum of Time.*

Suspended in this time warp, the Aboriginal person is
never more than a child.

*The simplicity of the aboriginal is in most cases the
untutored naiveté of the child rather than an inherent
mental deficiency or weakness.*

Aboriginal pre-contact life was often depicted by early colonial
artists. *(William Blake,* A Family of New South Wales,
National Library of Australia, PIC Drawer 4061 #S4296)

Such romanticism is considerably removed from the realities of life for Aboriginal people at the time. In 1949, many Aboriginal people couldn't vote and many had almost every aspect of their lives regulated – where they could live, what they could eat, where and when they could work. Aboriginal people were concerned about the state removing their children, the theft of their land, the destruction of their culture, heritage and language, cyclical poverty and the resultant diseases, starvation, illiteracy, and access to adequate services.

From the beginning of the British invasion right up to the present day, Aboriginal people have been strongly engaged in political activism, far from happy and passive about their treatment at the hands of the colonisers. There is no 'accepting of the fate', which is a recurrent characteristic in the noble-savage stereotype.

THE TAMED SAVAGE: EDDIE BURRUP AND THE PASTORALIST'S DAUGHTER

When someone sits down to create a fictional Aboriginal character they make choices based on their understanding of Aboriginal people, Aboriginal experience, Aboriginal worldviews, Aboriginal psychology and Aboriginal culture. The more deeply the writer understands these things, the more convincing the character they create will be; the less they understand, the more apparent the flaws in the construct. The choices made during this creative process can reveal much about how an outsider views their Aboriginal subject matter.

One example that draws this process out is painter Elizabeth Durack's construction of a *nom de brush*, Eddie Burrup.

Eddie Burrup's paintings first appeared through the Kimberley Fine Art/Durack Gallery in Broome. Three of his artworks were shown in *Native Title Now*, a 1996 exhibition open only to Indigenous artists; two were selected for inclusion in the Telstra 13th National Aboriginal and Torres Strait Islander Art Awards that same year.

Then, in the March 1997 issue of *Art Monthly*, Elizabeth Durack confessed to art critic Robert Smith that she was the artist behind the vibrant and hypnotically dramatic paintings attributed to an Aboriginal artist. Before Eddie Burrup, Durack had perhaps been best known as the illustrator of her sister Mary Durack's books, which she decorated with her distinctive squat-like, bestial, comical Aboriginal caricatures, but she was also recognised and respected as an artist in her own right.

Durack claimed that Burrup was an alter ego, implying that she saw the character as part of herself, a result of her own creative process. She chose Burrup as 'her medium', inspired by her life experience, including her relationships with Aboriginal people, and described Eddie as 'a synthesis of several Aboriginal men I have known'.

Durack developed a website that featured a constructed account of Eddie Burrup's life, explanations of his artworks, and praise by art critic Leon Deutsch. Eddie's 'words' appeared in Kriol but were interpreted by Durack, and the website was peppered with Eddie's totem, the sand crab.

According to the biography on the website, Eddie was born on a pastoral station in the Kimberley, given his name by the station's white owner, and sent to a Catholic Mission school before working in the cattle industry. He learned to paint during a stint in prison and since then had attained status as an Elder because of his skill at painting. Eddie was a strong supporter of the mining and the pastoral industries, and believed that the property he had been born on and had worked on, Yandeyarra, although returned to Aboriginal ownership, belonged to the whites. Eddie accepted European occupancy as a given, and talked of co-existence between black and white, stating that reconciliation had already occurred: 'Whitefella, blackfella, t'en 'm go two fella gissa-gissa arm-'n-arm.' And Eddie had praise for every white authority figure he'd encountered. Even his jailors were 'all very decent fella'.

Eddie came across as the kind of easygoing Aborigine, 'a good one', who worked hard and was happy to be dependent on the boss's benevolence. There was a notable lack of political content in Eddie's outlook and artwork. He had Dreamtime stories, Bible stories, and his *Sorry Business* painting was a memorial to the death of Princess Diana. Eddie also lamented that half-castes have no Dreaming: '… t'at why yella fella no got'm Tyukurrpa nothin' Dreaming'. He claimed that this placed the half-caste on the same footing as white people ("m allasome

Gudea noe-Gudea no get 'm Dreaming'). He also said that he was the only one who knew the Dreaming:

O'ny young fella 'e don' savy oldenday – 'e don' listen – 'e don' know nothin'-couldn'-care-less old fella Dreamin'time … 'e on'y allday watch'm video … 'e don' hear'm – on'y Eddie see'm Eddie 'ear'm.

In creating Eddie Burrup, Durack constructed the kind of affable, friendly, quirky Aboriginal that white people feel comfortable with, one who would be labelled as a 'real' one. She also created an Aboriginal person who knew his place and was comfortable with being taken care of by white people – and, moreover, one who lamented the end of the pastoral regime in which Aboriginal people were paid with rations rather than real wages.

Durack's construction of Eddie Burrup is made all the more interesting by her own family background, being a member of one of Australia's most prominent pastoral family dynasties, the daughter and heir of pioneers and squatters. The Durack family, led by Elizabeth's grandfather Patrick 'Patsy' Durack, were the first white people to take and occupy parts of the Kimberley. Mary Durack's *Kings in Grass Castles* chronicles the history of the family as they carved out and established their pastoral empire in Queensland and Western Australia, and describes how in 1881 the Durack family formed an expedition to go into the Kimberley region.

The book tells a typical colonial tale where punitive expeditions were justified because they taught the natives a lesson and ensured that valuable stock was safe. In it, Aboriginal people are depicted as impeding 'settlement' and 'civilisation'.

Another member of the Durack family, Jim Durack, wrote a long poem included in *Kings in Grass Castles*, in which he questions those who 'believe in kindness to the blacks', asking whether they would feel the same if their 'dusky friend' attacked them with a spear.

As a pastoral family, the Duracks were dependent upon the labour of Aboriginal people. In *Kings in Grass Castles*, Mary Durack describes her family's use of slave labour as a regime that is beneficial to Indigenous people. (Elizabeth's Eddie Burrup has this same high regard of the regime.)

> *All over the country, young natives like this were being recruited for station work and the old bogy of 'outside criticism' was being raised against the settlers for 'blackbirding aboriginal boys into slavery'. This was always a very touchy point with the station owners, for couched in certain terms their methods of native employment sounded as near to the general conception of slavery as might be. A black received no payment other than the basic necessities of life. His time off was at the convenience of the boss and his station activities. If he 'cleared out' he would be tracked down and brought back, while any other*

white man employing him without the consent of his original master would be breaking an unwritten law of the country. The station people, however, looked at the matter differently.

Durack uses her father's words to explain that perspective:

The black boy feels like a king in the saddle galloping over the plains where his fathers footed it for thousands of years, and what's more he likes his white boss, providing he is a man who knows his own mind, gives an order and sticks to it, even if it doesn't make sense to the blackfellow ... In tribal life they are used to having personal decisions made for them by acting in accordance with their ancient laws and are only confused if handled in a weak and indecisive manner and constantly given a choice of action. Our monetary system is still a mystery to the blackfellow. Even were there shops where he could spend the money he would not know the value of it ... The station people should be subsidised, not criticised for training such boys for useful work.

Later on, in the period from 1891 to 1893, the 'law' took over the policing on the frontier. Durack alludes to this:

Moreover, a daily living allowance of 2s 5d 'per knob' for all natives arrested as suspects and witnesses made it profitable to bring in as many as they could manage. Chained together neck to neck, wrist to wrist, the long lines of prisoners, men, women, and children, wound their miserable way over the bush tracks to receive sentence in Wyndham, Derby or Hall's Creek.

The vengeful, calculated and senseless killings of Aboriginal people were no longer carried out by punitive expeditions but had become legitimised as 'policing'. And the history of violence in the Kimberley area is not a thing of the far past; it continued during Elizabeth Durack's lifetime. The Forrest River Mission and Ernest River massacres took place in the Kimberleys in 1926. Bruce Elder describes the slaughter in his book *Blood on the Wattle*. Four white men (two mounted constables and two policemen) and two Aboriginal trackers moved through the camps of the area, killing indiscriminately as they went.

Their system was to move into a camp and shoot all the dogs and break all the spears before setting on the people.

The party established a base camp:

At one place on the Ernest River the posse constructed a main base from which they could attack nearby Aboriginal camps. They would ride out in the morning, move into a camp, capture as many of the inhabitants as possible, chain them together, and bring them back to the base camp. They would separate the men from the women. The men, still chained together, were led away from the camp to a lonely place on the edge of Forrest River where they were tied to a tree and shot.

The women, who had been chained to a nearby tree, were forced to witness the death and cremation of their menfolk. They were then marched for another 10 kilometres along the riverbank … they were all executed … and the bodies were burnt.

The gang moved along the Forrest River, which joins the Durack River, for a week, capturing, killing and burning bodies to conceal the evidence. Reverend Gribble, who investigated the massacre, made the following note:

We left the same day and reached the mission early next morning, and left for Ernest at noon. We went straight to the spot, being guided by Noble. Where the men had been done to death was a small tree to which the prisoners had evidently been fastened. Round this tree was a ledge of rock about a foot high. Dark stains were still visible, though great efforts had been made to clean up the declivity.

Men and women were slaughtered, their bodies burned to dispose of them. The perpetrators were police and the crime took place on a reserve. Reverend Gribble delivered a report on the murders to the Western Australian Parliament and this led to an investigation. Two of the men involved in the massacre were arrested for murder. However, they received sympathy and support from the local white community and were acquitted.

No doubt we are judging *Kings in Grass Castles* with contemporary eyes, but Mary Durack's account provides some valuable insights into the mindset of the time. The book remains in circulation today and forms part of the contemporary conversation about the story we tell about Australia's history, and we should interrogate the text in that light.

And although the book is written by her sister, we cannot separate Elizabeth Durack from the family history it recounts when we look at Eddie Burrup, and her explanations as to why and how she created an Aboriginal man like him. It is impossible to view her position and claims of friendship with and endorsement by Aboriginal people without remembering the backdrop of dispossession and frontier violence. For her part, Elizabeth Durack said she was startled by the response when the Eddie Burrup art fraud was revealed. She didn't seem to realise that she was not just painting but also creating a whole person, a persona, a psyche, a history. And she was also telling a story – the history of surviving the colonisation in which her family was so much a part.

Through Eddie Burrup, Durack, heir of the squat-tocracy, created an Aboriginal man and in doing so projected what she believed an Aboriginal person should feel about their land, how they should cope with colonial oppression, and how they should be able to survive the impacts of colonisation. She not only claimed to speak with the voice of the colonised, she also distanced herself from her own complicity in the colonial process by doing so.

Durack argued that the creation of her paintings was an act of reconciliation: 'I see it as working within the spirit of reconciliation ... arm in arm, within mutual respect, within progression together, within unity.' As her Eddie Burrup said: 'Whitefella, blackfella, t'en 'm go two fella gissa-gissa arm-'n-arm.'

In the article that unmasked Eddie Burrup, Robert Smith reads Durack's creation as an 'homage to Aboriginal Australia, but a concrete exemplar for reconciliation between two communities and two cultures'. But this is not a reconciliation between black and white Australia. This is about reconciling with one's own dark history, not by confronting it but by rewriting it. And it is a personal journey. As Durack told Smith:

At times over the last two – going on three – years since working in direct union with Eddie I have experienced feelings of tremendous happiness and a sense of deep fulfilment.

*This is about reconciling
with one's own dark history,
not by confronting it but
by rewriting it.*

Absent in this is any sense that 'reconciliation' has an element of reconciling *with* the Aboriginal people. Instead, as Durack sees things, it is a process that allows her to enter into the realms of the Aboriginal through her own imaginings about what Aboriginal people are like, what they experience and what they might want. Perhaps Durack was driven by a romanticised colonial nostalgia but her legacy – the Durack legacy – cannot be undone by imagining Aboriginal survivors who are adjusted and happy with the socio-economic poverty and lack of rights protection that colonisation and dispossession have left them with.

Art critic John McDonald has written:

> *If the invention of Eddie Burrup was psychologically necessary for the creation of these paintings, instead of attacking Durack's morals, perhaps we should admire her artistic ingenuity.*

McDonald rightly defends the artistic process and there is no doubt that, whatever Durack's motivation or inspiration, her 'Eddie Burrup' paintings are visually stunning, arguably the best work she ever produced.

But whatever the artistic process, it is Durack's need to construct an Aboriginal person as the artist of the work, and then enter the work in competitions solely for Aboriginal artists, that puts Durack on shakier moral and ethical ground. It takes her work from the realm of the artistic process and places it into the realm of cultural and colonial politics. As academic Julie Marcus observes, when it comes to Aboriginal art, non-Aboriginal critics have the greatest difficulty understanding issues of identity, ownership of cultural property, the concept of appropriation and artistic licence.

But perhaps all this talk about alter egos and reconciliation is more than an attempt to grapple with a colonial past and a reconciled future. Elizabeth Durack's daughter, Perpetua Hobcroft-Durack, claims to have planted the seed to create Eddie Burrup after the paintings had been finished. In an interview reproduced in an article by art expert and writer Susan McCulloch she revealed:

> *'I first said to Elizabeth,' says Hobcroft, 'one – as it turns out – fateful day in 1994 while looking at a stack of the arcane "Out of Mind" paintings. "Why are you doing this mad, wild work when the art cognoscenti will never look at it, let alone make any perceptive or intelligent comment concerning it? … If, however, this work had been done by an Aboriginal … then I believe it would be taken seriously … but you are so damn straight you could never exhibit under another name." Nothing more was said.*

Elizabeth did not respond and I'd forgotten about it when suddenly some hours later when we were walking by the river and talking of something else entirely she said, "I'm not totally against showing those morphological paintings under a nom de brush" ... It was then,' says Hobcroft, 'that the shadow of Eddie fell between us. He was just there, hat and all.'

This confession seems to undermine the assertions of those who came to Durack's defence when Eddie Burrup's true identity was revealed, those who said she was simply exercising creative licence. It raises the question of whether the creation of Eddie Burrup was simply a marketing technique, coming into being after the paintings had been executed. Did Durack seek simply to commodify her art by making it 'Aboriginal' and, through the creation of an 'authentic' Aboriginal persona, seek to appeal to white people's fascination with black people?

Durack knew exactly the kind of characteristics and traits to give her fictional Aboriginal person to make him seem authentic to potential buyers. She created an Aboriginal person whose views of colonisation reflected her own and, in turn, Eddie Burrup became a mirror that tells us much about Durack's own psychological battles and prejudices.

Another website now has a testament to Elizabeth Durack and her body of work. On it, the Eddie Burrup paintings are discussed and there is a page that talks about 'the detractors'. They are described as mostly 'from university arts or social science departments' who took on the use of the *nom de brush* with 'relish'. It laments that 'not one consulted a primary source; not one attempts to examine the art produced under the name of Eddie Burrup; not one considers the possibility that Eddie Burrup had valid alternative views to that of the mainstream'.

Elizabeth Durack's actions are complicated by the fact that she didn't appropriate anyone's art: the work was distinctive, unique and her own. And she wasn't 'outed'; she revealed herself. She also seemed to be of a different era, where the sensitivities around the use and appropriation of Aboriginal art and culture were not appreciated or respected.

This was a venture into an artistic cultural practice that appropriated Aboriginal history and experience without any subsequent self-reflection on the harm caused by originally masquerading as an Aboriginal artist in art competitions and exhibitions for Indigenous artists.

It is not true to say that the main detractors were academic elites. The deepest offence was to Aboriginal people – especially artists, including Aboriginal art expert, curator and artist Djon Mundine and artist Kaye Mundine. Wayne Bergmann (then acting head of the Kimberley Aboriginal Law and Cultural Centre) states in another article by Susan McCulloch:

> ... *in Aboriginal law, no-one can take another's work or another's identity. Miss Durack has failed to respect the very law and culture in which she claims empathy and understanding.*

THE MODERN NOBLE SAVAGE: MARLO MORGAN'S MUTANT MESSAGE

If Durack's Eddie Burrup is a compliant Aboriginal person, accepting of colonisation, it is interesting to look at an attempt to create the Australian Aboriginal as a modern-day noble savage, a purportedly 'positive stereotype'.

US author Marlo Morgan's best-selling New Age fantasy *Mutant Message Down Under* chronicles her trek through the Australian outback with a group of Aboriginal people, a 'lost tribe' who have retained their traditional ways of life.

The tribe kidnap Morgan to take her on the journey but she comes to understand that her abduction was no matter of chance. Rather, she was chosen because of her spiritual link with the leader of the tribe. The expedition culminates with her arrival at a secret, sacred jewel-encrusted cave in which the Dreamtime secrets have been kept. Morgan is cast in the role of saviour as she is given the message that she is to disperse among the other 'Mutants' (the supposed Aboriginal word for white people): the Earth is dying and the Indigenous peoples ('Real People') with it.

The stoic Aboriginal is not the hero of this story; that role is reserved for the white person and the Aboriginal person is the subject of deliverance. And since the white hero of the story is 'saving' the Aboriginal person, the underlying message is that the Aboriginal person is unable to save himself – he is powerless and has no agency.

But these Aboriginal people are not the Aboriginal people you would meet in community organisations in Redfern or Mount Druitt, on the outskirts of country towns, within the walls of a university or at your workplace. These Aboriginal people are a 'noble' breed, 'traditional'. Morgan even names them 'the Real People'. They are inevitably 'lost tribes' since such unaffected traditional existence was destroyed by colonisation long ago.

Few people, even Australians, understand Aboriginal culture well, if at all. It is easy to fool an audience. In her book, Morgan constantly creates aspects of cultural practices that could easily appeal to the New Age market. Her contrivances include possession of supernatural powers and displays of interconnectedness with nature achieved by reaching a higher consciousness. Morgan's most implausible example of those skills is telepathy, which, according to her, is commonplace in traditional Aboriginal culture. This skill extends to the ability of the desert-dwelling tribe to communicate with dolphins, and it is only one of the skills that derive from the purity of the 'Real People':

> *The reason ... that Real People can use telepathy is because above all they never tell a lie, not a small fabrication, not a partial truth, nor any gross unreal statement. No lies at all, so they have nothing to hide.*

Morgan's lost tribe engages in the practice of cannibalism. This is justified to her with a child-like noble primitivism:

'But cannibals never killed more in one day than they can eat. In your wars, thousands are killed in a few minutes.'

Morgan's text is littered with other invented cultural practices. She redefines the totemic system so that, rather than being a complex system of family bonds and interconnectedness with the environment, it becomes a quaint association with an animal that can be determined by the shadow of someone's nose. Among Morgan's inventions and distortions of Australian Aboriginal culture is the mixing of practices from other cultures. For example, there is a reference to a dream catcher, a cultural object of indigenous cultures from North America but found nowhere in Australia. (I'm reminded here of Eliza Fraser and her chroniclers who adapted her story to an American audience with reference to squaws, chiefs and wigwams.) Morgan also invents names for her Aboriginal companions: Tribal Elder, Big Music, Great Stone Hunter, Kindred to Large Animals and Bearer of Happiness. These names also seem to be more of a naive and misguided attempt to create Native American names; they certainly have no resonance with Aboriginal names anywhere in Australia.

If Morgan's portrayal is starting to sound incredible, note that her book was on the bestseller list for months in the United States. While HarperCollins discreetly categorised the book as 'fiction' when they released it in 2004, Morgan had self-published two earlier editions as non-fiction and promoted her book on the New Age market as an account of an actual experience. Morgan's introduction, which stated she could not reveal the name or location of the tribe for 'legal reasons', the back-cover endorsement of the authenticity of her work by Aboriginal Elder Burnum Burnum and her claims that she continued to contact her tribe through telepathy did little to present her book to the reader as fiction.

When it was published, *Mutant Message Down Under* stirred the ire of the Aboriginal community in Australia for distorting Aboriginal cultural practices. Morgan was accused of creating a misleading impression of Aboriginal people and their culture, and of being disrespectful in a manner that was offensive and distressing to Aboriginal people. In 1995, Noongar man Robert Eggington and Bardi Elder Paul Sampi travelled to Japan to confront Morgan as she addressed an audience there. In their statement at the event, they accused Morgan of being 'a fraud and spiritual thief', described her book as 'a fabricated New Age fantasy' and claimed her journey with 'the real people as nothing more than a hoax'.

I came across the book when I was living in the United States. It was 1994, the year it came out. I had several people ask me questions about it. Whether Aboriginal people were telepathic was a popular one – and it was frustrating that, with such little understanding of Aboriginal culture, this book that seemed to perpetuate so much misinformation had such a large audience.

The most manipulative aspect of Morgan's book is that she not only claims to have the voice to speak but that she also actively undermines the legitimacy of the voices of

Aboriginal people. On each occasion Morgan deals with an Aboriginal person who lives outside of her noble-savage paradigm, she treats them with insensitivity and prejudice, questioning their cultural authenticity.

She portrays urbanised Aboriginal people as being lesser than her 'Real People', and aware that they are less authentic and 'real':

> … but quite truthfully, they did not want to be reminded of their dark skin and the difference it represented. They hoped to marry someone of lighter color and eventually for their children to blend in.

No Aboriginal person is as pure, as untouched, as uncolonised as her fictitious tribe: '… every other tribe in Australia had submitted to the rule of the white government. [Her tribe] were the last of the holdouts.'

What Morgan is effectively saying is this: If Aboriginal people cannot perform this super-human feat of telepathy, they are not 'Real'. If they tell you there is no such super-human feat, they are lying or they are ignorant, they are not 'Real'. And in this way, Morgan silences her Aboriginal critics and privileges her own voice.

There are three characteristics of the noble savage as he (and it is almost always a man) has appeared in his original manifestations and contemporary adaptations like *Mutant Message Down Under*: his primitiveness, his passivity and his childishness.

The primitive is found in 'traditional' Indigenous

societies. The noble savage and his culture are untouched and untainted, a notion that is intertwined with naturalism, the idea that what is closest to nature is most pure. This is why, for a colonised society, the 'primitive' is often found in a secret lost tribe, preserved in time like a museum piece. The noble savage is not tempted by the commodities and conveniences European society has to offer, rejecting all possessions in favour of a simple life, communing with nature and developing a higher consciousness.

Because the noble savage is so inextricably linked to his natural habitat, he becomes a symbol of the health of the natural environment. According to this stereotype – and we see it in *Mutant Message Down Under* with the message given to Morgan – if the natural environment dies, then, naturally, the Aboriginal people die along with it. The noble savage is passive: he is unable, according to the romanticised view of this narrative, to adapt to new surroundings and circumstances, and so will instead perish. This ignores the ways in which many Aboriginal people have transformed their cultural practices to resist and survive dispossession. And it criticises any attempt to modernise Indigenous culture (the way all other cultures modernise and evolve) as lacking in authenticity or highlighting how the Indigenous culture is becoming extinct.

The nobility of the noble savage comes from a gallant, heroic acceptance of his fate, his knowledge that it is inevitable that his people's culture will die out and that they will perish with it. Morgan's 'Real People' not only accept their demise but also do so without complaint. They have no political agenda and express no anger about their treatment, nor do they engage in any acts of resistance. In the same way, Eddie Burrup is accepting of his fate and prefers the paternalistic arrangements of the ration days.

This 'noble savage' is one who does not bear the scars of the colonisation process: dispossession, genocide, rape, assault, poverty, disease. Just as Elizabeth Durack's constructed artist accepts and even embraces his colonisation and the role of the pastoral industry in his dispossession, Morgan's noble savages accept colonisation as inevitable and are resigned to disappearing in the wake of its onslaught. Any confrontational aspect of the Aboriginal presence is stripped away in this portrayal of the passive Indigenous person.

> *Any confrontational aspect*
> *of the Aboriginal presence*
> *is stripped away ...*

African-American scholar A Leon Higgenbotham in his book *Shades of Freedom* points out that those who are oppressed may have the capacity to be brave and noble like everyone else, but oppression itself is not what makes them brave and noble. He says:

> *... those who insist on seeing beauty in oppression often do so in order to assuage their guilt for contributing to that oppression. That is why the temptation to find beauty and nobility in suffering and oppression has a long and distinguished history.*

Aboriginal people, even as Elders or adults, are wrapped in an unspoiled innocence by the noble-savage construct. Without responsibility, without authority and without purpose, their childishness is expressed in the carefree and cheerful passing of the days. The Aboriginal life in *Mutant Message Down Under* is one with 'laughter all day long', where '[o]ur joyful day was ending with more laughter and jokes'.

Childishness is most clearly exhibited by the lack of agency that Aboriginal people have. Never able to deliver their own message, never concerned with politics, they are only able to be the beneficiaries of the actions of the white people willing to help them, willing to carry their message – as Morgan was asked to do.

WHAT HARM IS THERE IN A POSITIVE STEREOTYPE?

While there are many complaints about the negative images of Aboriginal people, there is less critique of the romanticism of the noble-savage ideology pervasive in texts and cinema. Such portrayals of Aboriginal people as a spiritually superior race, an incarnation of the noble savage, is often construed as a positive stereotype. But this raises a perplexing question: how do we treat this supposedly positive stereotype? Is Morgan, by portraying Aboriginal people in this light, doing them a favour? Is she – her self-promotion and deceptiveness notwithstanding – creating an image of Aboriginal people that may glean sympathy and support from non-Aboriginal people?

The noble-savage stereotype sits in stark contrast to the negative images of Aboriginal people that were created long before Eliza Fraser's captivity narrative – the black bogeyman, the unknown shadow who will lie, steal and molest. The idea of the untamed native who will lust after white women, seek to claim back his land, and be hostile and angry has pervaded since.

Media attention also perpetuates a negative perception of Aboriginal people by highlighting socio-economic problems or racial tensions. Through images of youths committing violence and engaging in criminal activity and anti-social, self-destructive behaviour, Aboriginal presence is often portrayed as being dangerous to the community, something to be feared.

There is little media coverage of the successful – and rather uneventful – day-to-day lives of Aboriginal people who participate in a broad range of community activities. These people and the community organisations they establish to do their work are hidden by images of out-of-control and violent Aboriginal people who are seen as lawless, without a sense of responsibility, as dangerous. Consequently, Aboriginal people are seen as a threat to peaceful and cohesive life in the city, a danger to the social fabric rather than making a contribution to it.

Popularising the noble savage, it has been argued, can counter these images by garnering sympathy and hence generating greater rights protections and equality. This strategy involves a political compromise and claims that the ends justify the means. If it suits the political agenda to assert this positive stereotype, the argument goes, what harm is done? What does it matter if rights are conveyed to the Aboriginal people because of perceived mystical characteristics or idealised traits?

While the short-term compromise may appear advantageous, the long-term outcome for rights protection based on the assertion of the noble-savage or positive stereotype is extremely detrimental to the Aboriginal community. If rights are granted based on sympathy towards a particular stereotype, those Aboriginal people who do not fit within that paradigm will be excluded, and considered inappropriate beneficiaries of these protections because they are not 'authentic'; they will be seen as not 'Real'. Those who do not embody the images of passivity, childishness and naturalism, who do not live lives based on an affinity with nature and devoid of any material possessions, who do not use quaint logic to deduce naive and simplistic understandings of the world around them, will be considered as being outside the set of worthy beneficiaries. And urban Aboriginal people, house-owning Aboriginal people, angry Aboriginal people, and Aboriginal people who do not speak their traditional languages will all fall outside of the Aboriginal people who are perceived to be deserving.

The traditional land of the Yorta Yorta nation is situated on the Murray River on both the New South Wales and Victorian sides. It unites the clans of the Wolithiga, the Moira, the Ulupna, the Bangerang, the Ngurai-illiam-wurrung, the Kwat Kwat, the Kaitheban and the Yalaba Yalaba clans. Europeans aggressively and violently invaded their traditional lands in the 1840s and this caused enormous alterations to the culture and economy of the Yorta Yorta people, who engaged in the processes of resisting the continual presence of non-Aboriginal people on their land and found ways to adapt to their new circumstances. It has been estimated that the Yorta Yorta population was reduced by 85 per cent within one generation of European invasion.

In 1992, the High Court of Australia recognised that Aboriginal people had a form of native title. The test was established in the *Mabo* case, which said that to prove native title, Aboriginal people had to have a continuous connection to land and show that nothing had been done by governments to extinguish their native title. The Yorta Yorta were the first people to lodge a native title claim after the *Native Title Act 1993* was passed, and it became the longest running native title case in Australian legal history. When Justice Olney of the Federal Court came to hear their claim in 1998, he approached the question of whether the Yorta Yorta still had native title by applying a test: the customs and traditions that existed at the time Europeans arrived on their lands formed the basis of a native title claim, and the extent to which these customs and traditions survived in the present would determine the extent to which native title survived.

He concluded:

The tide of history has indeed washed away any real acknowledgement of their traditional laws and any real observance of their traditional customs.

The court placed considerable emphasis on the meaning of the term 'traditional', requiring the Yorta Yorta claimants to prove that they had observed their laws and customs substantially uninterrupted from the time that European sovereignty was claimed until the present day. Where there had been a substantial change in laws and customs, they could no longer, according to the law, be described as 'traditional' laws.

The forced re-settlement of members of the Yorta Yorta nation onto reserves, the suppression of their language and cultural practices, their need to join the workforce for paid employment and their adoption of 'more orderly habits of industry', such as commercial farming and a settled lifestyle, were evidence to Justice Olney that, after only forty years of the colonisation process, the Yorta Yorta were no longer a 'traditional culture'. Justice Olney dismissed evidence of contemporary cultural activities, such as the protection of sacred sites and management of land and waters, finding that these were not practices that had occurred in pre-contact society. He determined that the Yorta Yorta had neither maintained the legally required connection to land nor their traditional laws and customs.

The applicants in the *Yorta Yorta* case were Aboriginal people who could clearly show that they were descendants of the Yorta Yorta nation; had knowledge of their language, oral histories and cultural stories; were aware of the locations of their sacred sites; and had evidence that they tended and cared for some of those sites. Yorta Yorta man Wayne Atkinson pointed out that his people were able to demonstrate that cultural continuity was the outcome of the forced changes that the 'tide of history' imposed.

In making findings of fact about the status of Aboriginal culture, the court relied on squatters' diaries, valuing this evidence more than the oral evidence of Yorta Yorta people about their cultures. Justice Olney seemed to place greater emphasis on the writings of pastoralist Edward Curr and missionary Daniel Matthews, who occupied the area during the 1850s, historical accounts written against a background of belief in white racial superiority and the idea that Aboriginal people were a dying race. These cultural biases did not seem to be acknowledged in Olney's examination of the evidence, and his privileging of white historical sources over traditional Aboriginal knowledge has been the cause of much criticism.

There is of course a tragedy in the fact that the more aggressive the impact of colonisation, the less able the dispossessed are to find a remedy, redress or recompense. Instead, the human rights abuses of the past that the Yorta Yorta people have suffered have been used against them to deprive them of recognition of their native title rights.

Underpinning the concept of native title is the assumption that an Aboriginal nation like the Yorta Yorta are not entitled to have their interests in their traditional land recognised unless they can show that the way the Yorta Yorta live today reflects the way in which their ancestors lived when they first had contact with Europeans. This creates a concept of native title that assumes that rights should be given to Aboriginal people only when they are more 'untouched', more 'primitive'.

Proving native title requires Aboriginal people to show the judge that they are as close to the 'traditional' Aboriginal person as they can be. To do this, they have to replicate the image of Aboriginality that is in the judge's mind. After all, judges make decisions from their own perspective. They have their own viewpoints, under-standings and preconceived ideas. But in this way, native title assumes that Aboriginality can be authentic only if it remains in a time warp, is stagnant, even against cataclysmic changes like those wreaked by colonisation. The 'frozen in time' approach adopted by Justice Olney failed to recognise the dynamic and changing nature of contemporary Aboriginal law and culture.

The frustration the Yorta Yorta people felt at the outcome of their case is understandable when you consider that they had to parade through the court to show that their culture was maintained in a way that an Anglo-Australian judge found acceptable. To be told by the court that, as a matter of law, their culture had 'disappeared into the mists of time' gave them a clear message: the legal system deemed that they were now no longer authentic or 'real'.

The Yorta Yorta appealed the decision to the full bench of the Federal Court in 2001 and then, in 2002, to the High Court. Both courts upheld Justice Olney's decision that the Yorta Yorta community had lost its character as a 'traditional' Aboriginal community.

Henry Atkinson is a Wolithiga Elder and spokesperson for the Yorta Yorta Nation Aboriginal Corporation Council of Elders. In an article he wrote in 2004, his response to the judge's findings was clear:

We've gone from wanting self-determination to the present day where a Judge sits and declares to one and all words to the effect that the tides of history have wiped out our continuity with our land and our ancestors, and as such we no longer existed as a people. Did he really expect us to be running around in loincloths with spears in our hands as is still depicted as the way the Indigenous people of this country live? What a load of rubbish. All societies evolve, some through their own progression and others because they are forced to.

'All societies evolve, some through their own progression and others because they are forced to.'

Like Marlo Morgan in *Mutant Message Down Under*, the court in the *Yorta Yorta* case refused to acknowledge the ability of Aboriginal people to live in modernity and still be Aboriginal. If Aboriginal people do not resemble the romanticised ideal of the untouched native, the 'noble savage', they are assumed to have lost their culture and, as a consequence, their native title rights.

It is dangerous to think that we can gain any political mileage by eliciting sympathy for the notion of Aboriginal people as noble savages. Those who peddle the noble-savage myth are not usually seeking to advance the situation of Aboriginal people; they are often more fascinated by what they can learn from Aboriginal culture to give them guidance about or meaning to their own lives. Morgan was not concerned with the rights of Aboriginal people when she wrote her book, and not all of the people who were attracted to the spiritual promises of her story were interested in bettering the position of the Aboriginal people. Morgan did not mention the issues of dispossession and land claims, assertions of sovereignty or human rights. Nor did she concern herself with an accurate portrayal of the lives of Aboriginal people. Moreover, she never sought acceptance by the Aboriginal people for her work; how they felt about her creation was irrelevant. Aboriginal people like Robert Eggington and Paul Sampi were not shy in attacking Morgan and her New Age followers, confronting her not only in Japan but also in the United States, condemning her actions and her words. Morgan's response to these men was glib: 'We are all together on this planet, but you are full of anger and hate. It is time to stop the hurt. It is time to join the rest of the world.'

The only thing that was important to Morgan was acceptance by and acknowledgement from the white community about what she had to say. The 'Real People' and their culture were merely a vehicle for her own message directed to her white readership. People enamoured with the noble-savage stereotype, those who for whatever reasons are attracted to the spiritual, mystical person, often express disappointment, disinterest or discomfort when they are faced with the contemporary reality of the angry urbanised Aboriginal man or woman, finding them unpalatable or unworthy of the sympathy that the image of the noble savage evoked. They seem to have similar frustrations about the way in which Aboriginal people on the fringes of towns like Alice Springs or Darwin or Broome seem to be caught up in social problems rather than living a spiritual life. This attitude is akin to assimilation, an attempt to make the Aborigine into an image of what he or she ought to be, rather than allowing them to live as they really are and accepting them that way.

Any short-term gains made by people's sympathy for the noble savage will be countered when that stereotype is shown to be a fiction. It is far better to say that Aboriginal people, *like all people*, are entitled to equal rights – to adequate health services, to protection of language, heritage and culture, to an education, to protection of their interests in land – not because they are noble, primitive or authentic, but because human rights are inherent and are held by Aboriginal people as much as they are by everyone else.

8

Telling Stories about Colonisation

JÓZEF TEODOR KONRAD KORZENIOWSKI was born in December 1857 in the Russian-occupied city of Berdyczów, Ukraine. His parents were Poles living in the Ukraine under tsarist autocracy. When Józef was a child, his father and mother were arrested for being involved with the Polish National Committee's anti-Russian activities. They and four-year-old Józef were exiled to the Northern Russian province of Vologda, where the harsh living conditions and climate took their toll. Both Józef's parents contracted tuberculosis – his mother dying of the disease in 1865, and his father in 1869.

At the age of twelve Józef became the ward of his maternal uncle, a landowner who lived in Kraków, Poland. In 1874, with his uncle's blessing – and as a way of avoiding conscription by the Russians – Józef travelled to Marseilles, France, and began his twenty-year career as a seaman. He served in the French and later the British Merchant Navy during the height of the British Empire. In 1886, Józef became a British citizen and formally changed his name to Joseph Conrad.

In 1890, Conrad's travels took him to the Belgian Congo, where he wrote his 'Congo Diary' that would later become his greatest novel, *Heart of Darkness*, first published in 1899. The harsh conditions of travelling to and working in the Congo Free State aggravated Conrad's ill health. He returned to England with the Congo having had a profound effect on him psychologically as well as physically.

Heart of Darkness tells the story of a sailor, Marlow, who travels upriver in the Congo. Marlow expresses a desire to go to Africa to his aunt, who procures for him a position as captain of a steamboat for the Company. He sets off for Africa and when he arrives at the first station he finds the blacks being poorly treated and ordered to do meaningless work by the whites. Marlow is sent on a mission to visit and, if necessary, retrieve the mysterious Kurtz, an enigmatic agent who has lost contact and reportedly fallen ill.

The journey takes several months and includes a trip along the coast, an overland trek to the Central Station, and finally the riverboat journey to Kurtz's outpost. During the entire expedition Marlow is struck by the mistreatment of the natives by the Company and its agents, the proliferation of disease, and the intimidating presence of the jungle. Marlow continues down the river on his steamboat with a crew of several whites and about twenty to thirty blacks. As he travels deeper into the jungle, his steamboat becomes surrounded by natives and a fog moves in. As the fog rises, the natives attack and Marlow's men fire back. Marlow's helmsman is hit and dies. Marlow blows the whistle and, mysteriously, all the savages retreat in fear.

On his travels, Marlow hears much of Kurtz – of his high moral principles, his effectiveness and his influence in the Company. When Marlow eventually arrives at Kurtz's station, Kurtz is very ill and needs to be taken back to England. But Kurtz does not want to go and it transpires that Kurtz had ordered the attack on the steamboat so that he would not be taken back home. Kurtz has set himself up as a sort of god to the natives he had once wanted to civilise and has become more savage than them, using violence and fear against the natives to motivate them to obtain more ivory.

Kurtz tries to escape but Marlow catches him and takes him back to the steamboat and they head back to England. While still on the river, Kurtz dies, repeating, 'The horror, the horror,' his reflection on what he has seen and who he has become. Before he passes away, Kurtz gives Marlow his papers, including an article he has written on bringing enlightenment and progress to the natives of the Congo. Kurtz has scribbled a postscript on the article: 'Exterminate all the brutes!' This is indicative of how far Kurtz has fallen from his original ideals, his isolation causing him to be exposed to the darkness within himself, and as a result he has gone mad.

When back in Europe, Marlow contacts Kurtz's fiancée. He gives her Kurtz's letters but does not reveal

Kurtz's terrifying last words or tell her what he had become before he died.

Conrad understood that colonisation was a mirror for the darkest nature of the coloniser. The journey into the Belgian Congo is symbolic of a journey towards our inner 'heart of darkness', and Conrad uses this context to explore the erosion of morality and the darker side of human nature, showing what happens when people are placed in situations where they have to rely on their baser instincts.

Conrad was also aware of the barbarity of colonisation. He refers to the naiveté of Europeans – particularly women – regarding the force needed for the process of colonisation, the brutal subjugation of the natives by the British traders and Belgian colonists, and the ways in which greed is as much a motive for colonisation as 'civilising the savages' is. And in the way Marlow hides the truth from Kurtz's bereaved fiancée, we see how stories of colonisation start to mask the unsettling and the unpleasant in favour of the heroic and the romantic.

… we see how stories of colonisation start to mask the unsettling and the unpleasant in favour of the heroic and the romantic.

A central theme of the novel is the eternal struggle between good and evil – not just between people but within ourselves. And these inner conflicts are most extreme in places where we feel most vulnerable. In this way, the frontier provides a setting in which to explore the deepest aspects of the human nature or the psyche of those who are seeking to conquer it. And in this setting, we can learn much more about those who are complicit in the process of colonisation than those who are its victims. Such insights provide a perspective through which to view colonial narratives.

THE NARRATIVE OF COLONISATION

Stories like Eliza Fraser's sought to reinforce the meta-narrative about Australia that was prevalent at the time she was shipwrecked: that the land was occupied by savages who had no attachment to it, who were a threat to European women and the Empire, and who needed to be Christianised or civilised.

Eliza Fraser's story was more than a boys'-own-adventure story or a ripping read. It also appealed to the public by depicting the treachery of blacks, made more fearful by their cannibalism, and the dangers they posed to vulnerable white women. It evoked the harshness of the Australian landscape, and hinted at the resilience of the white men who could – and would – see it tamed.

And, of course, there was something deeper going on. In 1836, the year of Eliza's shipwreck, the colonisation of

Australia had been underway for almost sixty years. Ours is a large continent and there was much resistance to the European presence. Stories like Eliza's offered a justification for the treatment and dispossession of Aboriginal people. Her tale of being captured by cannibals was a *cause célèbre* for the missionaries who used her experiences as evidence of the rightness of and need for the Christianising mission, and the Butchulla of Fraser Island connect her time among them with the start of the active process of being dispossessed of their land.

These stories became an important part of the colonising process because they illustrated the reasons given to justify the taking of Aboriginal land. They became part of the popular narrative of Australian history – the white man battling the elements and taming the wild land and the wild people upon it – for many years.

From the 1980s, particularly through the work of historians such as Henry Reynolds, Heather Goodall, Ann McGrath, Ann Curthoys, Lyndall Ryan and Peter Read, Aboriginal perspectives and experiences were being woven into the national narrative. These accounts inevitably challenged the previously dominant way of speaking about Australian history, which had remained largely silent about the fate of Australia's First Peoples. Through these counter-narratives, this wave of historians showed that, while victors write the history, that story can be challenged by dissenting voices and unpicked, until it ultimately frays at the edges.

But the emergence of these competing versions did not

happen without tenacious opposition. When Prime Minister Kevin Rudd delivered an apology to members of the Stolen Generations on 13 February 2008, it was an historic occasion. His speech indicated a seismic shift away from the position of the previous prime minister, John Howard, who had a personally held view that the history and experiences of Aboriginal people, particularly those of the Stolen Generations, should be downplayed and trivialised, if not hidden altogether.

The frontline for John Howard's attempt to imprint his ideological approach on the narrative of Australia's history was challenging the emergence of diverse voices. Under Howard's leadership, the counter-narrative that sought the inclusion of Indigenous voices was attacked and labelled as a 'black armband' view of history. Howard's 'white blindfold' sought to shut out anything about Australia's past that might be unpleasant or a source of guilt, restoring the 'white man conquering the savage land' legend.

The tension between the 'black armband' and the 'white blindfold' became known as the 'history wars' and then the 'culture wars', and they raged through the fierce debates about the telling of history, the squabbling about numbers killed on the frontier, whether there were massacres of Aboriginal people or not, whether Aboriginal children were 'stolen' or removed for their own good, and the proper legal definition of genocide.

These culture wars were not about Aboriginal history. Aboriginal experience and perspectives remain unchanged by semantic and numerical debates by academics. They were, instead, a battle about white history and, more importantly, white identity. It was a conversation about the kind of country Australia should be and what the dominant national narrative should say about Australians. These culture wars were also much more than ideological battles between public intellectuals, academics and the opinion writers in newspapers. In her book *How Institutions Think*, Mary Douglas writes about how a society often feels the need to control the memory of its members, to have them forget experiences incompatible with its own righteous image, and evokes images that are complimentary to itself. And storytelling is a powerful mechanism by which to advance this agenda.

Stories like Eliza Fraser's, told to advance the colonial agenda, find their way into institutions, including legal systems. They are used to sanction the removal of Aboriginal people from their lands and Aboriginal children from their families. They are used to legalise the theft of Aboriginal lands and dictate the terms on which Aboriginal people can recover their rights.

Even our benchmark cases, our victories, cannot be separated from the colonial context in which they have been created.

LEGAL FICTIONS

When Captain Arthur Phillip planted the flag at Sydney Cove in 1788, he wasn't claiming the land for the British to take it away from the Aboriginal people; he was making sure the French didn't claim it first. (Jean-François de Galaup, comte de Lapérouse, was hanging around on an expedition with two ships.) International law had developed a doctrine of discovery that dictated the rules by which European colonial powers could claim territory around the world. The ceremony of raising the flag might have been symbolic but it was one of the acts recognised as an assertion of a prior claim against other conquering nations who might be eyeing off the same turf.

At the time Phillip planted that flag he didn't consider the land *terra nullius*. He had instructions to deal with the natives with 'amity and kindness', which means that everyone expected they would be there. But their rights to land, their systems of law and governance, and their customs and traditions were ignored and undermined by the tenacious colonisation process. And although those land rights were not recognised, Aboriginal and Torres Strait Islander people kept asserting them. One example was the Yirrkala bark petitions that the Yolngu presented to the Australian Parliament in 1963 as a way of asserting their interests in their traditional land against the incursions of mining activities. Not surprisingly, the Yolngu did not just wait for an answer but pursued their claim through the Australian courts in what would become known as the *Gove Land Rights case (Milirrpum v. Nabalco Pty Ltd)*. In 1971 the case came before Justice Blackburn of the Supreme Court of the Northern Territory.

Justice Blackburn was a highly esteemed judge, later becoming Chief Justice of the Australian Capital Territory Supreme Court and appointed to the Federal Court. He was a clever man who knew that Aboriginal people had existed at the time Australia was claimed by the British, and that they had their own laws and governance systems. He knew that the Indigenous people had a connection to their land; it just wasn't one that the British or the Australian legal system could recognise: the law treated this land as *terra nullius*. And since Justice Blackburn was bound to apply the law as it was before him, he had to apply that to the Yolngu. The result was that the mining leases were upheld and the court reaffirmed that the Yolgnu had no interest in their land because 'the doctrine of communal native title … does not form, and never has formed, part of the law of any part of the law of any part of Australia'. The decision also saw the concept of *terra nullius* entrenched in Australian law as a legal fiction. Everyone knew there were Aboriginal and Torres Strait Islander people, and that they had laws and customs, but the law created a fiction – a story – that they didn't. So the law told a story about colonisation. And Justice Blackburn was not in a position to change that.

But in 1982 three Torres Strait Islander men started a long legal journey that ended ten years later with the *Mabo* case. This time the High Court did what Justice Blackburn couldn't, and changed Australian law by overturning the doctrine of *terra nullius* and finding that there was a native title interest that could survive in certain circumstances.

The language of the court was interesting, and in the leading judgement, Justice Brennan eloquently set out the test of the extent to which the Australian legal system can overturn long-standing traditions such as *terra nullius*.

Brennan is a humanitarian with a deep sympathy for Indigenous Australians, but this was not the basis for his judgement. Rather, he based it on a formal legal approach, stressing that the role of the law is not to freely adopt the standards of justice if that would threaten the 'skeleton of principle' that gives the body of our law its shape and internal consistency. As legal academic Sandra Berns notes in her book *To Speak as a Judge*, Brennan navigated a thin line between making the law just and not undermining the property rights structure as it stood. The judgement was an articulation of how far the law would go, a statement about how much institutional change can be tolerated.

Brennan went on to say that there should not be unquestioning adherence to law if it offends 'the values of justice and human rights'. He also acknowledged that the facts as we know them now do not sit with the 'absence of law' or barbarian theory underpinning the colonial reception of the common law of England. He further noted that it was the acts of government, not the common law, that had taken land from Indigenous people. The law wasn't wrong; the law had been incorrectly applied. It should have acknowledged native title; it didn't. And now the *Mabo* case has rectified that.

So the *Mabo* case tells another story about colonisation. It overturned the legal fiction of *terra nullius* and replaced it with a narrative that treated Australia as settled. That Australia was 'settled' is not an uncontested narrative. Aboriginal and Torres Strait Islander people characterise that part of the national story as one of invasion, not settlement.

The law tells our national story as much as historians, prime ministers and novelists do. Law can be complicit in storytelling because, in the process of determining and applying law, judges have to reconcile conflicting arguments and come to a conclusion by relying on the credibility of the witnesses and other evidence that has been accepted. This is a human exercise and therefore always susceptible to bias, prejudice, preconceived ideas and existing worldviews.

PSYCHOLOGICAL *TERRA NULLIUS*

In her novel *The Secret River*, Kate Grenville tells of the Thornhill family that moves from England to the new penal colony of New South Wales after the husband is convicted of stealing. At the end of the book, when the family has staked its piece of land, struggled and persevered, and made a small fortune from trade, they build a colonial mansion as a testament to their wealth. The foundations of the house are built over the carved stone image of a large fish, which had been created during ceremonies performed by the Aboriginal clans who had lived in the area for thousands of years but had now been pushed away, massacred or had died of illness.

Grenville, unlike her fictional family, understands that the land that brought the Thornhills such riches was acquired through an act of stealing. Her symbolism is a striking reminder of the history that lies beneath our modern Australian state and of the ways in which that history has sometimes been deliberately suppressed to give the impression of more noble beginnings. When a colonising culture seeks to find its place in a country that is not theirs, how do they deal with the presence of the original inhabitants? Do they seek to silence the Aboriginal inhabitants so that their own story of conquest will not be challenged or undermined? Or do they find a way to incorporate the narratives of those they have displaced into their own story?

There are no absolute truths when it comes to history. It is a process, a conversation, a constantly altering story. As Inga Clendinnen writes in her book *True Stories*:

> *To consolidate good history made out of true stories we need time, and peace, and we need the will. We also need to keep in mind that truth is a direction and an aspiration, not a condition.*

History, then, is no longer just one romanticised story – it becomes a series of competing narratives, brought to life by different groups whose experiences are diverse and often challenge the dominant story that a country seeks to tell itself about its history. As philosopher Michel Foucault once wrote:

> *... the central issue ... [is] to discover who does the speaking, the positions and viewpoints from which they speak, the institutions which prompt people to speak about it and which store and distribute the things that are said.*

The Butchulla's presence and account of their time with Eliza Fraser and their subsequent dispossession provides an example of how these voices challenge the storyteller and their agenda. For the most part, the Butchulla are unnamed as part of the Eliza Fraser captivity narrative. They are a shadowy threat; too savage to be characters, personalities or people. But they have their own interpretation of their contact with Eliza. Their account not only demonstrates the type of cultural conflict and misunderstanding that would plague black–white relations in the years to come, but also shows the way in which the dominant narrative – the other story we tell about our history – silences other perspectives.

In his essay 'Mind and Earth', Carl Jung observes:

> *Certain Australian Aborigines assert that one cannot conquer foreign soil, because in it there dwell strange ancestor-spirits who reincarnate themselves in the new born. There is a great psychological truth in this. The foreign land assimilates the conqueror.*

Like Kurtz in *Heart of Darkness*, colonists might come to conquer but in the end they struggle with the inevitable impact their environment and situation will have on them.

Stories like Eliza Fraser's, in the way Aboriginal people are constructed and the roles they play, reveal much more about the motives of the person writing the story than the Aboriginal people in it. In the same way, the obsession with cannibalism explains more about the European psyche when vulnerable than it tells us about the cultural practices of Aboriginal people. The construction of a *nom de brush* like Eddie Burrup reveals more about the person who made him up than it does about the lives of Aboriginal people. And even the way in which Aboriginal people are romanticised in the noble-savage stereotype shows more about the needs and desires of non-Aboriginal people than it does about the spirituality of Aboriginal people.

In these stories, we learn much more about the coloniser than we ever learn about the colonised, but by looking at them through different lenses and different perspectives we begin to appreciate the complexities and nuances of our own history.

9

Happily Ever After

THE MORE I looked into Eliza's story, the more it intrigued me – and the more Eliza intrigued me. From where we view her now, she is an enigmatic figure, elusive no matter how much you read about her.

It would be easy to dismiss Eliza as a racist but I think she is more complex than that. She was resilient, surviving a shipwreck that killed several others (all men). And she was able to capitalise on her circumstances in a society where there were few options for women. She was entrepreneurial and a survivor. Yes, she believed in her own cultural and racial superiority, considered Aboriginal people to be barbaric and savage, was dismissive of their knowledge and technology, and was ungrateful for their help. But in a lot of these attitudes, Eliza was simply a product of her time and reflected the prevailing views of the day.

Much of the way Eliza's story was told by others paid little heed to the complex woman she was. Instead, she became a symbol of the ambitions and worldviews of others. In their hands, her story turned into, at various times, one of domination, conquest, psyche, and religious and racial ideologies. Everyone had their own agenda in telling Eliza's story, exploiting her and her circumstances for their own gain, their own missionary zeal, their own greed and their own desire for land.

Eliza's story – and captivity narratives in general – served useful political and nationalistic purposes. They unified colonists in what they saw as the rightness of the way they behaved towards Indigenous people. In this way, Eliza's story came to symbolise worldviews that would in time shape future relationships with the land and the Aboriginal people. These worldviews were transferred to laws and policies that demanded that the land and the savage tribes that inhabit it be tamed. The 'natives' had to be civilised and Christianised, Aboriginal people had to be assimilated (forcibly if need be) to ensure they had the benefits of 'civilisation' – and all this with the under-lying assumption of white racial superiority. Aboriginal society had nothing to offer and nothing of value that was worth saving or protecting.

But captivity narratives like Eliza's are just one way to tell the story about first contact. There are others that describe alternative approaches to relationships with Indigenous people and those that offer a promise of a different future, a different dominant relationship.

Lieutenant William Dawes came to Sydney on the First Fleet in 1788. He was an astronomer but first came ashore as an engineer and surveyor. He helped to build the colony, constructing streets and surveying the surrounding countryside. He maintained his interest in the skies and began to study the stars from the part of the harbour foreshore that is now known as Dawes Point. Although the Indigenous people of the area were cautious about entering the colony, many came to his hut and it was seen as a welcoming place, a safe haven where knowledge and friendship were shared.

Unlike most of his contemporaries, Lieutenant William Dawes was willing to engage with Indigenous people and curious to learn from them. *(Image by Rod Blackford. Courtesy of the Bureau of Meteorology)*

Instead of being scared and dismissive as Eliza was, Dawes was curious about this country and its Aboriginal people. He was a man of science who wanted to understand his new surroundings. He engaged with the Aboriginal people, particularly a young girl named Patyegarang, from whom he learned the local language and knowledge of tides, food, medicine, Aboriginal perspectives and stories about the stars. We know this because he kept a diary that chronicled his time in the colony and recorded snippets of conversation and other observations.

Kate Grenville's novel *The Lieutenant* is inspired by the relationship between William Dawes and Patyegarang. Her hero, Daniel Rooke, describes his anticipation of what he might learn from this strange new land and its mysterious, elusive inhabitants: 'He was watching one universe in the act of encountering another.' Rooke's colleague, Silk, had an 'impulse … to make the strange familiar'; Rooke's instinct was to seek 'that strangeness and lose himself in it'.

'He was watching one universe in the act of encountering another.'

But curious co-existence was not the norm in the colony. Conflict increased between the First Peoples and the new arrivals as it became increasingly evident that the colonists intended to stay. In those earliest days of the colony, European diseases had decimated the populations of the Sydney tribes. Violent conflict occurred as a result of the mistreatment of Aboriginal women and the stealing of Indigenous people's tools and weapons. The colonists' permanent structures and activities were increasingly encroaching on the clans' traditional food sources.

In 1790 Governor Phillip's gamekeeper was speared when he upset local Aboriginal men because of the way he was exploiting their hunting grounds. As retribution, Phillip ordered several marines, including Dawes, to capture two Aboriginal men and sever the heads of ten more. After intervention from senior officers, he lowered this to the capture of six Aboriginal men, and if they couldn't be captured, they would be shot. Dawes refused to participate. He was arrested but after discussions with Reverend Richard Johnson agreed to take part.

The expedition, fortunately, was a failure. They didn't even find any Aboriginal people. Dawes then publicly declared that he regretted taking part, a stance that affected his relationship with Governor Phillip. Dawes had dreamed of finding a life in Australia for himself and applied to stay in the colony, perhaps becoming a farmer. Governor Phillip agreed on a few conditions. One was that Dawes apologise for his public comments condemning the punitive expedition. Dawes refused.

Dawes left the colony in 1791 and arrived back in England in 1792. He went to Sierra Leone that same year, and would become governor there at various times between 1792 and 1803. He also became involved with the international anti-slavery movement. In June 1799, Dawes gave evidence before a committee of the House of Lords when they were considering legislation to limit the slave trade. In 1813, he went to Antigua, where he was a correspondent of the Church Missionary Society and also established schools for the children of slaves.

Dawes allows us another way not only to view first contact but also to think about what might have been. What if William Dawes had been the story that sparked the national imagination in the way that Eliza Fraser had? It would not have changed the outcome of Australia being colonised, but the relationships with the land and with the Aboriginal people could have been very different if Dawes's approach of mutual respect and exchange of knowledge had served as a foundation. For Dawes, his experience of being close to Indigenous people deepened both his understanding of the world around him as well as his understanding of a common humanity.

And I can't help but wonder what the world we live in would look like today if the ideas Dawes brought with him had continued as a pattern of engagement. Could these principles have led to a treaty, a negotiation of a balance of rights between those of the Indigenous people and those of the colonising power? Could what the colonists learned from the knowledge Indigenous people had of foods, medicines and weather patterns have increased their ability to adapt to life in Australia? Could there have been a deeper integration of Indigenous culture and creative practice into the emerging dominant Australian culture? Could there have been a deeper respect for the integrity of Aboriginal and Torres Strait Islander families and their kinship connections? Could we have created a society that more deeply valued the concepts of reciprocity and respect for Elders? Could we have had a society that respected the ability of Aboriginal people to make decisions over the key things that affect their lives? Could we have a more compassionate view about all of humanity? If they followed the example set by Dawes, colonists would have felt very differently about this country and Indigenous people, and they would have understood both the land and its people in a much deeper way.

And what can these alternative approaches mean for our society today? What would happen if we rejected Eliza Fraser's separation of 'us' and 'them', with the inevitable domination of one over the other, and embraced Dawes's approach of mutual respect and shared knowledge? Is it too late for Australians to more deeply embrace the Aboriginal heritage that is still deeply rooted into the country in which they live? What would happen if we used traditional knowledge to understand climate cycles? What if we sought to rely more on the medicines and rich food sources that are part of our natural environment? What if we applied traditional knowledge about ecosystems to our lands and our waters? What if we used fire technology in a more purposeful way? All of these changes would allow us to understand the world around us better – just like Dawes sought to do. And if all this knowledge to improve our health and the health of our environment was valued, it could be integrated – and embraced – by Australians in a meaningful way.

A humanitarian approach that respects Indigenous perspectives and knowledge could lead to an Australia where all Australians have an investment in Indigenous history and culture. It wouldn't be a case of 'us' and 'them'; rather, Indigenous culture would be seen as a central part of Australian culture. It could lead to an inclusive nationalism that celebrates diverse perspectives and experiences. An inclusive approach would not only improve relationships with Indigenous people but also improve the way we understand multicultural communities and other marginalised groups, particularly asylum seekers. And within this inclusive nationalism we can acknowledge that there is no one dominant national narrative but a range of concurrent, competing and conflicting stories that reflect the diversity of backgrounds and perspectives within Australian society.

Of course, it goes more deeply than just the stories we tell, as Eliza's own story shows. Changed values and approaches and new narratives should all work towards more fundamental changes in policies, laws and structures.

In 2014, the Butchulla had their claim of native title over Fraser Island granted. This acknowledged what was clear when Eliza Fraser came into their world that fateful day in 1836 – that the land was, and always would be, Aboriginal land. The Butchulla continue to proffer what they offered Eliza and her compatriots when they found themselves stranded – co-existence and a sharing of country and resources. It is a future that Eliza couldn't have imagined but here it is.

Acknowledgements

Janet Hutchinson, Madonna Duffy, Terri-Ann White, Fiona Foley, Kat Wright (Senior Ranger on Fraser Island), Geoff Scott, Sue Abbey and Kerry Davies, Ian See, Blue Lucine, Michael McDaniel, and Raema Behrendt.

References

Articles and books

Aboriginal and Torres Strait Islander Women's Task Force on Violence, *Aboriginal and Torres Strait Islander Women's Task Force on Violence Report*, Department of Aboriginal and Torres Strait Islander Policy and Development, Queensland, 1999.

Alexander, Michael, *Mrs. Fraser on the Fatal Shore*, Michael Joseph, London, 1971.

Anonymous, *Tales of The Thousand and One Nights*, Penguin Classics, New York, 1973. c. 1706.

Arens, William, *The Man-Eating Myth: Anthropology and Anthropophagy*, Oxford University Press, Oxford, London, 1979.

Atkinson, Henry, 'Yorta Yorta Co-operative Land Management Agreement: Impact on the Yorta Yorta Nation', [2004] *Indigenous Law Bulletin* 56; (2004) 6(5) *Indigenous Law Bulletin* 23.

Atkinson, Judy, 'Violence against Aboriginal Women: Reconstitution of Community Law – the Way Forward', *Aboriginal Law Bulletin*, vol. 2, no. 46, 1990, pp. 6–9.

—— 'Book Review: *Aboriginal Women and Violence* by Audrey Bolger', *Aboriginal Law Bulletin*, vol. 2, no. 54, 1992.

—— 'We Al-li. Womens Forum. Making a Difference', *Queensland Youth Affairs Conference Report*, 1994.

Australian Institute of Aboriginal and Torres Strait Islander Studies, *Encyclopaedia of Aboriginal Australia*, Aboriginal Studies Press, Canberra, 1994.

Barker, Francis, Peter Hulme and Margaret Iversen (eds), *Cannibalism and the Colonial World*, Cambridge University Press, Cambridge, 1998.

Barrett, Charles, *White Blackfellows: The Strange Adventures of Europeans Who Lived among Savages*, Hallcraft Publishing, Melbourne, 1948.

Beasley, Jack, *The Rage for Life: The Work of Katharine Susannah Prichard*, Current Book Distributors, Sydney, 1964.

Berns, Sandra, *To Speak as a Judge: Difference, Voice, Power*, Ashgate, Dartmouth, 1999.

Bird, Delys (ed.), *Katharine Susannah Prichard: Stories, Journalism and Essays*, University of Queensland Press (UQP), St Lucia, 2000.

Bolger, Audrey, *Aboriginal Women and Violence*, Australian National University North Australia Research Unit, Darwin, 1991.

Brady, Veronica, 'A Properly Appointed Humanism? *A Fringe of Leaves* and the Aborigines', in John McLaren (ed.), *Prophet from the Desert: Critical Essays on Patrick White*, Red Hill Press, Melbourne, 1995.

Brown, David, David Neil, David Ferrier and David Weisbrot, *Criminal Laws*, The Federation Press, Annandale, 1990.

Brown, Paula and Donald Tuzin, *The Ethnography of Cannibalism*, Society for Psychological Anthropology, Washington, 1983.

Bunyan, John, *The Pilgrim's Progress*, Penguin Books, Ringwood, 1965. c. 1678.

Carter, Edie, *Aboriginal Women Speak Out*, Adelaide Rape Crisis Centre Inc., Adelaide, 1987.

Carter, Sarah, *Capturing Women: The Manipulation of Cultural Imagery in Canada's Prairie West*, McGill-Queen's University Press, Montreal and Kingston, 1997.

Clarke, Marcus, *For the Term of His Natural Life*, Macmillan, London, 1904. c. 1899.

Clendinnen, Inga, *True Stories*, ABC Books, Sydney, 1999.

Clune, Frank, *Jimmy Governor, the True Story*, Angus & Robertson, Sydney, 1978.

Conrad, Joseph, *Heart of Darkness*, Penguin Books, London, 1991. c. 1899.

Curtis, John, *Shipwreck of the Stirling Castle*, George Virtue, Ivy Lane, London, 1838.

Daniels, Kay, *Convict Women*, Allen & Unwin, St Leonards, 1998.

Davies, Brian, *The Life of Jimmy Governor*, Ure Smith, Sydney, 1979.

Davison, Liam, *The White Woman*, UQP, St Lucia, 1994.

Dawes, William, *William Dawes: notebooks on the Aboriginal language of Sydney: a facsimile version of the notebooks from 1790–1791 on the Sydney language written by William Dawes and others*, SOAS, London, 2009.

Dawson, Barbara, *In the Eye of the Beholder: What Six Nineteenth-century Women Tell Us about Indigenous Authority and Identity*, ANU Press, Canberra, 2014.

Defoe, Daniel, *Robinson Crusoe*, WW Norton & Co., London and New York, 1994. c. 1719.

de Montaigne, Michel, 'On Cannibalism', in *Collected Essays*, MA Streech (tr.), Penguin Books, London, 1991. c. 1575.

Docker, John, *In a Critical Condition*, Penguin Books, Ringwood, 1984.

Dostoyevsky, Fyodor, *The Idiot*, Penguin Books, London and New York, 1955. c. 1869.

Douglas, Mary, *How Institutions Think*, Syracuse University Press, Syracuse, NY, 1986.

Dryden, John, *The Conquest of Granada in Two Parts*, Henry Henningman, London, 1673.

Durack, Mary, *Kings in Grass Castles*, Bantam, Sydney, 1959.

Edwards, Coral and Peter Read (eds), *The Lost Children: Thirteen Australians Taken from Their Aboriginal Families Tell of the Struggle to Find Their Natural Parents*, Doubleday, Sydney, 1989.

Elder, Bruce, *Blood on the Wattle: Massacres and Maltreatment of Aboriginal Australians since 1788*, New Holland Publishers, Sydney, 1998.

Flannery, Tim, *The Explorers*, Text Publishing, Melbourne, 1998.

Fraser, Eliza, *Narrative of the Capture, Sufferings, and Miraculous Escape of Mrs. Eliza Fraser*, Charles S Webb, New York, 1837.

Freud, Sigmund, *Totem and Taboo: Some Points of Agreement between the Mental Lives of Savages and Neurotics*, Routledge, London, 1965. c. 1950.

Gale, Fay (ed.), *Women's Role in Aboriginal Society* (3rd edn), Australian Institute of Aboriginal Studies, Canberra, 1986.

Gibbings, Robert, *John Graham, Convict, 1824: An Historical Narrative*, JM Dent & Sons, London, 1937.

Goodall, Heather, *From Invasion to Embassy: Land in Aboriginal Politics in New South Wales, 1770–1972*, Allen & Unwin, St Leonards, 1996.

Gunn, Mrs Aeneas, *We of the Never-Never*, Random House, Milsons Point, 1990. c. 1908.

Hanson, Neil, *The Custom of the Sea*, Doubleday, London and Sydney, 1999.

Healy, Chris, *From the Ruins of Colonialism*, Cambridge University Press, Cambridge, 1997.

Heseltine, Harry, *Acquainted with the Night*, Townsville Foundation for Australian Literary Studies, Townsville, 1979.

Hughes, Robert, *The Fatal Shore*, Pan Books, London, 1988. c. 1987.

Human Rights and Equal Opportunity Commission, *Racist Violence: Report of the National Inquiry into Racist Violence in Australia*, Australian Government Publishing Service, Canberra, 1991.

—— *Bringing Them Home: A Guide to the Findings and Recommendations of the National Inquiry into the Separation of Aboriginal and Torres Strait Islander Children from Their Families*, HREOC, Sydney, 1997.

James, Bruce, 'The Politics of Envy', *The Sydney Morning Herald*, 15 April 2000.

Janke, Terri, *Our Culture Our Future: Report on Australian Indigenous Cultural and Intellectual Property Rights*, Michael Frankel, Sydney, 1998.

Joint Women's Action, *What Hope Justice?*, Joint Women's Action, Canberra, 1974.

Jung, Carl, 'Mind and Earth', in *Collected Works of CG Jung*, vol. 10, Princeton University Press, Princeton, 1970. c. 1927.

Keneally, Thomas, *The Chant of Jimmie Blacksmith*, Angus & Robertson, Sydney, Melbourne and London, 1974.

Laurie, Rowena, *Speak Out Speak Strong: Researching the Needs of Aboriginal Women in Custody*, Aboriginal Justice Advisory Council, 26 October 2004.

Lestringant, Frank, *Cannibals*, University of California Press, Berkeley, 1997.

Limbers, Rosaleen A, *Katharine Susannah Prichard*, Little Hills Press, Sydney, 1981.

Lumholtz, Carl, *Among Cannibals: An Account of Four Years' Travels in Australia and of Camp Life with the Aborigines of Queensland*, ANU Press, Canberra, 1980. c. 1889.

Marx, Karl, *Capital: A Critique of Political Economy*, Workers Literature Bureau, Melbourne, 1944. c. 1867.

Mason, HGB, *Darkest West Australia: A Treatise Bearing on the Habits and Customs of the Aborigines and the Solution of 'The Native Question'; A Guide to Out-Back Travellers*, Hocking, Kalgoorlie, 1909.

McCulloch, Susan, 'What's the Fuss?', *The Australian Magazine*, 5–6 July 1997.

McCulloch-Uehlin, Susan, 'When Is a Fake Not a Fake?', *The Weekend Australian*, 15–16 January 2000.

McDonald, John, 'Durack – Let's Look at the Big Picture', *The Sydney Morning Herald*, 26 May 2000.

McGrath, Ann, *Born in the Cattle: Aborigines in Cattle Country*, Allen & Unwin, Sydney, 1987.

McNiven, Ian, Lynette Russell and Kay Schaffer (eds), *Constructions of Colonialism: Perspectives on Eliza Fraser's Shipwreck*, Leicester University Press, London and New York, 1998.

Miller, James, *Koori, a Will to Win: The Heroic Resistance, Survival and Triumph of Black Australia*, Angus & Robertson, Sydney and London, 1985.

Miller, Olga, *Legends of Fraser Island*, Rigby Heinemann, Port Melbourne, 1994.

Mouzos, Jenny, 'New Statistics Highlight High Homicide Rate for Indigenous Women', *Indigenous Law Bulletin*, vol. 4, no. 25, 1999, pp. 16–17.

Mundine, Djon, 'The Land Is Full of Signs: Central North East Arnhem Land Art', in Howard Morphy and Margo Smith Boles, *Art from the Land: Dialogues with the Kluge–Ruhe Collection of Australian Aboriginal Art*, University of Virginia, Charlottesville, 1999.

Pickering, MP, 'Cannibalism among Aborigines: A Critical Review of the Literary Evidence', unpublished doctoral thesis, Australian National University, Canberra, 1985.

Poe, Edgar Allen, 'Narrative of A Gordon Pym', in *The Complete Tales and Poems of Edgar Allan Poe*, Vintage, New York, 1975. c. 1838.

Prichard, Katherine Susannah, *Coonardoo*, WW Norton & Co., New York, 1930.

Read, Peter, *A Rape of the Soul So Profound: The Return of the Stolen Generations*, Allen & Unwin, St Leonards, 1999.

Reece, Bob, *Daisy Bates: Great Dame of the Desert*, National Library of Australia, Canberra, 2007.

Reece, RHW, *Aborigines and Colonists: Aborigines and Colonial Society in New South Wales in the 1830s and 1840s*, Sydney University Press, Sydney, 1974.

Reynolds, Henry, *The Other Side of the Frontier*, Penguin Books, Ringwood, 1995.

—— *Frontier: Aborigines, Settlers and Land*, Allen & Unwin, St Leonards, 1996.

—— *Why Weren't We Told?*, Penguin Books, Ringwood, 1999.

Rolfe, Patricia (ed.), *Clotted Rot for Clots and Rotters*, Wildcat Press, Sydney, 1980.

Rousseau, Jean-Jacques, *Émile*, Barbara Foxley (tr.), Everyman's Library, Melbourne, 1911. c. 1793.

Ryan, Yoni, *Coonardoo by Katherine Susannah Prichard*, Department of Discussion Programs, Council of Adult Education, Melbourne, 1986.

Sartore, Richard L, *Humans Eating Humans: The Dark Shadow of Cannibalism*, Cross Roads Books, Notre Dame, 1994.

Schaffer, Kay, *In the Wake of First Contact: The Eliza Fraser Stories*, Cambridge University Press, Cambridge, New York and Melbourne, 1995.

—— 'Whose Cannibalism?: Consumption, Incorporation and the Colonial Body', in Máire ní Fhlathúin (ed.), *The Legacy of Colonialism*, Galway University Press, Galway, 1998.

Simpson, AW Brian, *Cannibalism and the Common Law*, Chicago University Press, Chicago, 1984.

Smith, Robert, 'The Incarnations of Eddie Burrup', *Art Monthly Australia*, March 1997.

Sturt, Charles, *Two Expeditions into the Interior during the Years 1828, 1829, 1830 and 1831 – with Observations on the Soil, Climate and General Resources of the Colony of New South Wales*, 1833.

Summers, Anne, *Damned Whores and God's Police*, Penguin, Ringwood, 1994. c. 1975.

Swift, Jonathan, *Irish Tracts 1728–1733*, Basil Blackwell, Oxford, 1955.

Tannahill, Reay, *Flesh and Blood: A History of the Cannibal Complex*, Hamilton, London, 1975.

Thieme, John, *Postcolonial Contexts: Writing Back to the Canon*, Continuum, London, 2001.

White, Isobel (ed.), *Daisy Bates: The Native Tribes of Western Australia*, National Library of Australia, Canberra, 1985.

White, Patrick, *A Fringe of Leaves*, Vintage, London and Sydney, 1997. c. 1976.

Williams, RM, *I Once Met a Man*, Angus & Robertson, Sydney, 1996.

Wilson, Gavin, *Escape Artists: Modernists in the Tropics*, Cairns Regional Gallery, Cairns, 1998.

Wonderful Australia in Pictures, Colorgravure Publications (Herald & Weekly Times), Melbourne, 1949.

Legal cases

Mabo et al. v. Queensland [No.2] (1992) 175 CLR 1.

Members of the Yorta Yorta Aboriginal Community v. Victoria. 214 CLR 422 ('the Yorta Yorta case').

Milirrpum v. Nabalco Pty Ltd, (1971) 17 FLR 141 ('the Gove land rights case').

R v. Burt Lane, Ronald Hunt and Reggie Smith, Supreme Court of the Northern Territory, 1980.

R v. Dennis Narjic, Supreme Court of the Northern Territory, 1988.

R v. Dudley and Stephens (1884) 14 QBD 273 (QB).

R v. Mingkilli, Martin and Mintuma, Supreme Court of the Northern Territory, 1991.

Also by Larissa Behrendt

LEGACY

**Winner of the 2010 Victorian Premier's Literary
Award – Prize for Indigenous Writing**

Simone Harlowe is young and clever, an Aboriginal lawyer
straddling two lives and two cultures while studying at Harvard.
Her family life back in Sydney is defined by her complex
relationship with her father, Tony, a prominent Aboriginal
rights activist.

As Simone juggles the challenges of a modern woman's
life – career, family, friends and relationships – her father is
confronting his own uncomfortable truths as his secret double
life implodes. Can Simone accept him for the man he is and
forgive him for the man he's not?

'In a balanced and absorbing way, Behrendt juxtaposes
the importance of Aboriginal sovereignty alongside the
challenges facing individual Aborigines. It was a joy to
read.' *The Courier-Mail*

ISBN 978 0 7022 3733 1

UQP

HOME

'A stunning first novel.' Kate Grenville

Candice is a young woman setting out on her first visit to the traditional land of her Aboriginal grandmother. When she arrives at 'the place where the two rivers meet', the twentieth century falls away and the story of Candice's family comes to life. Here, in 1918, her grandmother Garibooli was taken from her family.

Garibooli is sent to work as a housemaid, but marriage soon offers escape from the terror of the master's nighttime visits. Her displacement carries into the lives of her seven children – their stories witness to the impact of orphanage life and the consequences of having dark skin in postwar Australia. Vividly rekindled, the lives of her family point the direction home for Candice.

'Behrendt brilliantly explores the subtleties of race and identity in a palpable way.' *The Age*

ISBN 978 0 7022 3407 1

UQP

Lightning Source UK Ltd.
Milton Keynes UK
UKHW021331130720
366460UK00007B/1267